Table of Contents

Preface 5
Acknowledgments 10
Introduction 11

Chapter 1
A Jim Crow Childhood 16

Chapter 2
Setting the Stage: *Brown v. Board* 23

Chapter 3
The Blossom Plan 29

Chapter 4
Opposition Mounts 35

Chapter 5
The First Day 42

Chapter 6
Showdown 49

Chapter 7
Going Off to War 57

Chapter 8
The Lost Year 65

Chapter 9
The Next Steps 74

Chapter 10
Homecoming 81

Epilogue 89
Endnotes 91
Bibliography 94

Nine Little Niggers

Nine little niggers in Little Rock School?
Arkansas citizens start mob-rule.

Integration the White forbids,
"No little niggers sit with our kids!"

God's White chillum from the class-room run –
Nine little niggers? No, not one!

The Federal Court removed the ban –
Let little niggers in – if they can!

The Governor posted the National Guard,
The school-house doors were locked and barred,

But nine little niggers were smuggled in,
Then had to fly to save their skin.

But citizens who the law would thwart
Stand in contempt of the Federal Court,

And National Guard and State Police
In Little Rock failed to keep the peace,

And the President said to Little Rock,
"Arkansas won't put back the clock!"

Now Federal Troops move in to show
All God's chillum to school may go.

Deep South Governors urge a stand –
"Halt integration in Dixieland!"

Will nine little niggers set off the spark?
The eyes of the world are on Little Rock, Ark.

Will citizens now include lynch law
In the sovereign rights of Arkansas?

Or will they heed the order terse,
"Lawless assemblies must disperse"?

Federal troops the law enforce –
All little niggers take the High School course,

Till Little Rock, Ark., accepts the view
That colored folk are citizens too.

A racist poem composed as a "new school song"
for Little Rock Central High School, 1957

Preface

The best of American History is made up of people . . . who experience a moment of revelation that inspires them to fight against injustice.

—Juan Williams
Author of *Eyes on the Prize – America's Civil Rights Years, 1954-1965*

IT BEGAN WITH A PHONE CALL. I sat nervously in the teachers' lounge with a sense of trepidation. What do I say? What if she says no? These questions ran through my head as I approached what would become one of the most exciting adventures of my teaching career. It was the summer of 1998 and I had just finished my first year teaching at Mt. Zion High School. Mt. Zion is a small village with a population of approximately six thousand located in central Illinois, just southeast of Decatur. At the time, I was teaching a contemporary American history course entitled, History Since '45, a semester-long look at the people, places, and events that have shaped our nation's history since the end of World War II. One of the units in my curriculum included the civil rights movement.

My earliest experience regarding race occurred when I was nine years of age. I grew up in a very small town called Rutland, Illinois. Rutland is one of the countless, all-white, rural, farming communities scattered throughout the north/central part of the state. I distinctly remember meeting a new kid in elementary school named Pete Walls. Pete was black, but at that time I was not conscious of a color difference. Pete and I shared a love of *Star Wars*, and that's all that mattered to me. I find it interesting that our views on race do not seem to materialize until we are older and after being influenced by our home environment. Children learn certain behaviors by watching their parents' reactions in various situations and I was no different. I was taught by my parents to respect those around me, so at the time Pete was just another one of my friends. His color didn't matter.

It was around this same time period, in 1983, that NBC aired a made-for-television movie, simply titled *Kennedy*. Famous actor Martin Sheen starred in the title role as a tribute to the life and times of our thirty-fifth president on the anniversary of his death twenty years earlier. In one particular scene from that film, a young mother is walking with her children along a street in Birmingham, Alabama. Two men are standing along the sidewalk as they pass by. Suddenly, one of the men trips the woman and she falls to the ground. Both men begin kicking her violently, hitting her head repeatedly with a tire iron. The camera pans down the street to reveal two policemen witnessing the event who smile, turn, and walk away. The men who beat her stand laughing with their beer-drinking buddies across the street.

As a nine-year-old child, I found these images to be very confusing. "Why were those men beating her?" I thought. "Why did the policemen just turn and walk away?" I remember being upset as I watched this scene of children crying beside their mother as she lay in a pool of her own blood. Later, I had a conversation with my mother who watched the program with me. "Why did they do that to her?" I asked. She told me that back in the 1960s, some people inflicted pain and suffering on others simply because they had a different skin color. Of course, that answer did not make much sense to me at the time, but it did spark my interest in this period of history.

As I went from elementary school to junior high, my love of history deepened. Most of that was due to an inspiring social studies teacher named Brian Hipes who brought the subject matter to life for me and my classmates. Still, at the time, both textbooks and teachers rarely mentioned anything beyond Rosa Parks, Dr. Martin Luther King Jr., and the Civil Rights Act. As a student, all I recalled was segregation was something "bad" that happened in the South and was "fixed" by something called the civil rights movement. Of course, my views on this would evolve over time, and a perfect opportunity arose as I entered high school.

Growing up as a "child of the 80s," I was heavily influenced by what I saw on television. In the summer of 1988, PBS ran a six-part series called *Eyes on the Prize*. This was my first real look at the civil rights movement through the eyes of the participants themselves. I watched the first installment and was riveted to the TV and even recorded the remainder of the series. I remember watching it over and over again, engrossed in the stories of Emmett Till's murder, the Montgomery bus boycott, the sit-in movement, the freedom rides, and, of course, something called the Little Rock Crisis.

I often referred to the *Eyes on the Prize* series in reports I wrote for both high school and college history courses. Later, as I assumed the role of a teacher at Mt. Zion, I noticed my department had a copy of the *Eyes on the Prize* series and I was *expected* to show parts of it during class as part of my curriculum. I was ecstatic—this could not get any better, I thought.

When February of 1998 rolled around, the time had come for me to teach the civil rights movement. I already used a clip from *Eyes on the Prize* when discussing the Emmett Till murder, so I wanted to do something different when covering the Little Rock integration crisis. The trouble was I did not know much about the event. The clip from *Eyes on the Prize* on Little Rock was brief, as was information in the textbook. A mere paragraph was not enough time to devote to a topic I thought was so important for my students to learn. I remember having a conversation with one of our science teachers, Mr. Junius Futrell, who had an interesting perspective on this case. He remembered the incident as a boy and related his thoughts to me. I did not learn until years later that Junius was the grandson of former Arkansas governor Junius Futrell, his namesake. As interesting as his stories were, there just was not enough material to fill up a forty-eight-minute class period.

Time was running out and I was getting worried. As it happened, a former college roommate from the Chicago area, Brandon Doty, was coming down to visit for a couple of days. He was excited to observe my classroom and even offered to team-teach a lesson with me. "I have a great idea for you," I told him before he arrived. "Why don't you search the internet for information regarding the Little Rock Crisis and you can help me teach that." "Perfect," he replied. Unbeknownst to me, there was a big celebration in 1997 in Little Rock to commemorate the fortieth anniversary of the integration at Central High. A companion website had been set up that focused on all aspects of the event. Brandon brought information from the website with him and as we read through it, I was amazed at the detailed information that was not contained in the textbook or even the *Eyes on the Prize* program. The integration in Little Rock seemed to be a monumental historical event, I thought. Why had I never heard of this before?

The lesson went well, and the students and I both learned something about the Little Rock Crisis. One of the pages on the website was titled "The Little Rock Nine Today" and offered a brief description of each of the Nine and their careers, as well as listed their current residence. I was astonished to see that one of them, Thelma Mothershed Wair, lived in Belleville, Illinois. A suburb of St. Louis, Belleville is only a couple of hours away from Mt. Zion. I immediately started running a scenario through my head. What if I could get her to come speak to my students? The thought remained in the back of my mind as I taught the rest of the semester.

As soon as school was out for the summer and the schedule for the next year was set, I saw I would be teaching History Since '45 again that fall. I remembered my earlier thought regarding Mrs. Mothershed Wair and walked down to the teachers' lounge to use one of the few phones where personal calls were allowed. I called information first. They gave me the number for a Fred Wair, the only person by that name in Belleville. It has to be the right number, I thought. I called and waited for what seemed like an eternity for the connection to be made. I sat nervously as the phone rang on the other end and then a woman's soft voice answered, "Hello?" I took a chance. "Is this Thelma Mothershed Wair?" I asked. By this time, my heart was pounding so loudly I was sure she could hear it over the phone. "Yes, it is," she answered. I nearly dropped the phone. "Do you speak about your experience at Little Rock to students?" I asked. "Yes," she answered. "Would you be able to come to Mt. Zion and speak to my students?" "Sure!" she replied. We talked for a few more minutes about the details concerning her visit. As I hung up the receiver, I immediately had a feeling this would be one of the most important phone calls of my life.

Thelma Mothershed Wair meets the author for the first time at Mt. Zion High School in September 1998.

When the day to meet my students' first guest speaker finally arrived, I paced anxiously by the front door of the school while my class waited upstairs. After what seemed like an eternity, I noticed a short woman walking slowly with a cane. I greeted her at the door. "Thelma Mothershed Wair, I presume?" She paused, looked up at me, and smiled. "Yes, you must be Rich. It's very nice to meet you." At that time, our school did not have an elevator, so I assisted her up the stairs. Each step seemed to require huge effort on her part, and soon she apologized for her slow pace. She revealed her affliction with multiple sclerosis and how it limited her mobility. We chatted briefly as we made our way up the stairs and down the hall to my classroom. Thelma's husband, Fred, followed behind, carrying pictures of the Nine which we displayed in the classroom. Thelma took her place at my podium and I went to the back of the room. "Hello, students," she began. "My name is Thelma Mothershed Wair, and I'm one of the Little Rock Nine."

Over the next two years, Thelma continued to come and speak to my students about her experiences until Fred's health declined and he could no longer drive her. Wanting to stay in touch with Thelma, I decided if she could not come to Mt. Zion, I would take my students to her. This began in the fall of 2001, when I took a busload of students to her assisted living facility in Belleville. Later, Thelma moved back to Little Rock and over the next several years I began taking students on end-of-the-year field trips to visit with her. In May 2015, I had the opportunity to take some students to nearby Springfield, Illinois, to meet with Thelma. She and the surviving members of the Little Rock

Thelma Mothershed Wair meets with Mt. Zion High School students (The First Ladies) during her trip to Springfield, Illinois, in May 2015.

Nine were in Illinois to receive the annual Lincoln Leadership Award sponsored by the Abraham Lincoln Presidential Library and Museum.

Having the opportunity to befriend this icon of the civil rights movement has been one of the greatest experiences of my career as an educator and has expanded my knowledge of African American history. I now offer a class entitled the African-American Experience, in which I teach students about this country's troubled racial past and help them search for ways of reconciliation and understanding. It has also inspired me to become more involved with the African American community. I currently sit on the board of directors for the African American Cultural and Genealogical Society of Illinois Inc. Museum, based in Decatur. Each year, my students create exhibits for the museum through a community service project.

It is my hope in writing this book that the reader will learn how one young woman's determination in the face of adversity helped break down racial barriers. Thelma's story is one of inspiration, teaching us we can overcome the obstacles placed in our path if we have faith and courage. By viewing civil rights history through the lens of Thelma Mothershed Wair's life, it becomes apparent that, although this country's struggle for civil rights is far from over, we have made great progress—thanks to Thelma and the other members of the Little Rock Nine, who bravely walked up the steps of Central High School and into the pages of history.

Acknowledgments

A WORK OF THIS KIND cannot be accomplished without the help of individuals and groups and there are several I wish to thank as I worked on this project for ten years. First of all, I wish to thank my family and colleagues for their support over the years. It has meant a lot to me to have such good friends that have shown a genuine interest in my work. The love of writing was instilled in me at an early age by two very special teachers to whom I owe a lot—Judy Bennington and Vickie Fitzgerald. This type of research requires the assistance of trained professionals, and I am indebted to the staff at the Little Rock Central High School National Historic Site in Little Rock, Arkansas; the Eisenhower Presidential Library in Abilene, Kansas; and the University of Arkansas at Little Rock Library. I appreciate the generosity and patience I was shown at those places while conducting my research. I would also like to thank those who accompanied me on my numerous trips to Little Rock including my parents Don and Rose Hansen, Gina Day, Karen Penn, Janet Hogan, Pam Roberts, Matthew Trusner, Cathy Having, Jake Koniak, Marty Smith, Kathy Gissler, Marisa Gissler, Michele Hocking, Emily Bone, Katelyn Marshall, Tayler Anderson, Dianne Hansen, and Bob and Bev Dondeville. I also appreciate the support of my good friend and general manager of Little Rock's Riverfront Steakhouse, Donnie Rieathbaum. He runs a fabulous establishment with the best steaks in the area and a top-notch staff. Every time I have hosted an event at the restaurant with my students, Donnie has always taken special care of us to ensure a memorable evening. A special thank you definitely goes to Rhonda Davis, a close friend who graciously gave of her time as she painstakingly proofread my manuscript and helped me with revisions. Richard Trigg at the Jefferson National Parks Association as well as Anne Burns at the Donning Company Publishers deserve a lot of credit for their help in assisting me to prepare my manuscript for publication.

I also wish to thank the members of the Mothershed family for welcoming me into their homes and allowing me to tell their story. Of course, none of this would have been possible without the patience, love, and support I received from Thelma over the years. She is one of the most positive and inspiring people I have ever had the privilege to meet. I am so glad her story is finally being told and I look forward to sharing her experiences with future students through this book. And finally, I thank God for setting me on the path of education and giving me the opportunity to meet Thelma. I am truly blessed.

Richard J. Hansen
October 2016

Introduction

Negroes are not responsible for the kind of men and women they are. It is their nature, and they cannot possibly rid themselves of that, any more than skunks and polecats can cast away their abominable scent glands and the outrageous odors they emit. It is not everybody who cares, however, to have a large number of skunks and polecats in the community.

—Dr. Robert W. Shufeldt
Author of *The Negro – A Menace to American Civilization*

IN THE LAST DECADES of the nineteenth century, race relations in America had undergone a profound change. Following the Civil War, the Reconstruction period of the 1860s and 1870s had provided significant, but short-lived, opportunities for blacks across the South. The system of slavery, which had lasted in America for over two centuries, was dead. Republicans in Congress had appropriated money to build churches, schools, and hospitals in the South through the Freedman's Bureau. Blacks were being elected to positions of power in civic and state government. Constitutional amendments banned slavery, granted citizenship status to former slaves, and allowed for freedmen to vote. Education was now available for the first time to freedmen and freedwomen.

During Reconstruction, Arkansas perceived itself as a progressive state in regard to race relations. Indeed, many blacks living in neighboring states such as Mississippi and Louisiana considered Arkansas a "promised land."[1] Between 1870 and 1890, a growing black middle class in Arkansas afforded itself more economic independence from whites and shielded itself from some of the worst Jim Crow discrimination.[2] There were black ministers, doctors, lawyers, businessmen, and teachers. The University of Arkansas even admitted black students when it opened in 1872. However, to avoid embarrassment and controversy among the faculty, these students were taught separately by the president after normal school hours.[3]

This perception that Arkansas was a haven for blacks in the Reconstruction era hid the reality that most blacks in Arkansas were not members of the middle class, but rather they were the wage laborers making up the working class. While this group did have access to education, school terms were shortened to accommodate the agricultural system and inferior buildings and instruction hindered black advancement among the working class. The black middle class was aware of this disparity, and while offended by their exclusion from public accommodations and classification as second-rate citizens, they nevertheless advised their poorer brothers and sisters to remain in the state. Other southern states were viewed as far worse for blacks than Arkansas.[4]

Several factors were responsible for limiting black progress, not only in Arkansas, but throughout the South in the late 1800s. During this "Redemption" period, sharecropping had emerged as a system of farming between freedmen and their former masters. Under this agreement, the former slave worked the land for a small wage and was forced to pay the owner for rental of tools and a place to live. Usually, the whole wage went toward tool rental and freedmen found themselves once again in a state of poverty and at the mercy of the plantation owner.

Legal restrictions also hindered black advancement. Black Codes of behavior were included in new southern state constitutions to keep former slaves "in their place." These Black Codes restricted social interaction between the races, enacted curfews on blacks, and required poll taxes to be paid in order to vote. Section Five of the Arkansas Black Code, enacted in 1867, stated that "no negro or mulatto shall be admitted to attend any public school in this state, except such schools as may be established exclusively for colored persons."[5] Despite their blatant unconstitutionality, these Black Codes were allowed to stand. The violence perpetrated by supremacist groups like the Ku Klux Klan to enforce the Black Codes was largely ignored by the federal government in favor of self-regulation, known as "home rule" in the South.

Southern states also began passing measures which mandated separate accommodations along racial lines. John Tillman, an Arkansas state senator, introduced a bill in 1891 which required railroads to provide separate white and black coaches and waiting rooms.[6] These state measures would ultimately lead to a Supreme Court showdown in 1896 over separate railcar accommodations. The *Plessy v. Ferguson* case legitimized this type of discrimination, also known as "Jim Crow" segregation, making "separate but equal" the law of the land for the next sixty years.[7]

Social interaction along the color line was seen as taboo and could incur the harshest penalties. The Ku Klux Klan, and later lynch mobs, acted outside of the law and used means of intimidation and murder to enforce these new racial boundaries of the Redemption. The lynching rate escalated throughout the South in the 1890s and early 1900s. During this period, Arkansas had the sixth-highest lynching rate of all the states. Two hundred fourteen lynchings occurred in Arkansas, of which 182 (or 85 percent) of the victims were black.[8]

As America entered a new century, whites effectively removed rights granted to blacks during Reconstruction. Besides legal and extra-legal efforts on the part of racist whites, popular culture began to reflect this new attitude toward blacks. The image of poor, but happy, blacks was seen as a gross caricature of the disenfranchised black person. There were "coon" songs, "Little Black Sambo" stories, minstrel shows, and even games involving the "jolly darkie." Stereotyped images reduced blacks to exaggerated physical features involving kinky hair, thick lips, and bulging white eyes.[9] "Scientific" research of the period promoted this stereotype. One of the most highly regarded studies of blacks in the early twentieth century is a book by Robert Shufeldt, who published his work *The Negro – A Menace to American Civilization* in 1907. In it, Shufeldt, a retired army doctor, asserts that lynchings "will continue to occur in the United States of America just so long as there is a negro left here alive, and there is a white woman living for him to assault. He can no more help his instincts than he is responsible for the color of his skin."[10]

This negative attitude towards blacks only intensified as black veterans returned home from fighting in France during the First World War. Having experienced relaxed racial acceptance in France, their presence fed into southern white fears of black male aggression and social equality among the races. The Great Migration of blacks to northern states following the war exacerbated racial conflict. In Arkansas, this was especially evident in the Delta region where blacks were high in number. In one instance in Pine Bluff, a white lynch mob tied a black veteran to a tree and shot him nearly fifty times for allegedly insulting a white woman.[11]

Race riots were on the rise in post-World War I America, particularly in the immediate aftermath. The year 1919 saw numerous bloody race riots across the country, with outbreaks from Cadwell, Georgia, to Washington, DC; Corbin, Kentucky, to Ellsville, Mississippi; and Omaha, Nebraska, to Chicago, Illinois. The last (and bloodiest) race riot of the "Red Summer" of 1919 took place in the community of Elaine, Arkansas. What began on September 30 as a misunderstanding between white police and sharecroppers outside of a black church resulted in a white officer being shot and killed. Over the next three days, hundreds of innocent blacks would be slaughtered by locals as well as troops called in from nearby Camp Pike.[12]

America in the 1920s also witnessed increased anti-immigrant attitudes, similar in nature to anti-black sentiments. Catholic and Jewish immigrants had been arriving by the thousands each year, and Americans began to feel their way of life was being threatened. A renewed Ku Klux Klan, which promoted 100 percent Americanism and white supremacy, boasted more membership at this time than in any other era. Little Rock's Klan Chapter #1 enlisted 7,800 of Arkansas's 25,000 knights.[13] The group met weekly in a building on the corner of Fourth and Main Streets. Before the KKK's mass march in Washington, DC, in

1925, Little Rock hosted its own Klan parade downtown the year prior, which attracted some 10,000 members.[14] The capital of Arkansas also became the national headquarters for the Women of the Ku Klux Klan.

With the KKK in town, blacks in Little Rock and surrounding communities were living in a state of constant fear. This intensified in May 1927 with the lynching of John Carter. Carter was accused of attacking two white women on the outskirts of Little Rock. After being strung up in a tree and shot over two-hundred times by a mob, Carter's body was strapped to a car's rear bumper and dragged through the streets of Little Rock. The mob stopped at the corner of West Ninth Street and Broadway, where they burned Carter's mutilated body on a makeshift funeral pyre of pews stolen from a local black church. Only the presence of National Guardsmen sent in by Governor John Martineau was able to disperse the crowd which numbered more than a thousand.[15] Just a few months after John Carter was brutally lynched, another event captured the attention of thousands of people in Little Rock. This time, the place was the corner of 14th and Park Streets and the occasion was a dedication ceremony for a brand new high school—Little Rock Central High.

***

Bloomburg, Texas, was a sleepy farming community about twenty-five miles south of Texarkana with a population of around one-thousand people and eight to ten storefronts. One could pass the time admiring the lotus blooms while fishing at one of the many ponds or walking leisurely on red-soiled dirt roads along the endless forests. A hint of pine coming from the nearby paper mill, which processed pulp wood, filled the air. It was a quiet town where everyone knew everyone else. It was here the Mothershed family would have its roots.

As with most black families of the era, the local church played a central role in the lives of black Americans. In the community of Bloomburg, Shady Grove Baptist Church became the foundation for the Mothershed family. It was unthinkable for the family to miss a Sunday service, especially since the family patriarch, Oscar Mothershed, was the minister at Shady Grove. Oscar's fame in the area was not limited to his preaching abilities. He also was responsible for founding the Bloomburg Academy—a school for African Americans who lived in the area.[16] The Mothershed family always placed a high premium on the value of an education. Little did Oscar know that his great-granddaughter would one day be thrust into the national spotlight while trying to attend a white school.

It was in the very early years of the twentieth century that Oscar's son, Charlie Mothershed, and his wife, Ollie Mae Rosetta "Mama Ollie" Johnson-Mothershed, purchased a fifty-four-acre farm outside of Bloomburg. There,

Charlie and Ollie Mae began their family. Together the union produced twelve children, including Thelma's father, Arlevia Leander, or A. L. The Mothersheds had an orchard that produced fruit used for canning. In addition, they grew peas, potatoes, corn, cotton, peanuts, and watermelon. Corn was used for feeding the animals and making corn meal while cotton was sold as a cash crop to sustain their farm. In the 1930s, Charlie bought another farm a few miles north of the family farm. This new piece of land contained a lot of timber, which Charlie cleared out on a daily basis.[17]

Overwork and exposure to smoke from the burning brush caused Charlie to suffer health problems and in 1937, he died, leaving Ollie Mae to raise their children on her own. A strict disciplinarian, Ollie Mae kept her children in line. Assistance came from her extended church family as well as her own mother, Emma June Johnson. A former slave, Emma June was a strong-willed, yet gentle woman who lived in a log cabin in Caney, Arkansas, a short distance from Bloomburg. Emma June was the only great-grandparent Thelma ever knew.[18]

Despite having a large farm to work and a family to feed, Ollie Mae had no problem getting hired help on the farm, in part due to her reputation as an excellent cook. Many neighbors offered help in return for a good home-cooked meal. Assistance also came from her grandchildren, including Thelma's brothers, Gilbert and Michael. They stayed with their grandmother every summer for about a month, getting up early every morning to a breakfast of biscuits and gravy, ham, rice, grits, and scrambled eggs before heading out with their uncles to pick cotton and fruit, bale hay, and help out with other chores on the farm.[19]

About 150 miles to the northeast, in Lonoke County, Thelma's maternal grandparents, George and Caroline "Carrie" Moore, owned an eighty-acre farm where they raised their fourteen children, including Thelma's mother, Hosanna Claire. George's family had migrated to Arkansas from North Carolina. Heading a family with modest means, George and Carrie had invested everything they had into their children's futures. Like the Mothersheds, obtaining an education was extremely important to the Moore family, and to that end, George and Carrie saved their money and sent their children to church-supported high schools and colleges where the children could work to help pay part of their tuition. Their daughter, Hosanna Claire, attended high school at Nelson High in Lonoke County before enrolling at Jarvis Christian College in Hawkins, Texas. It was at Jarvis College that Hosanna Claire met a young man named A. L. Mothershed. Soon the friendship blossomed into love and A. L. asked Hosanna Claire to be his wife. The two were married on May 27, 1936. It was the beginning of a long and prosperous union blessed with six children—Lois, Grace, Gilbert, Michael, Karen, and, of course, Thelma.[20]

CHAPTER 1
A Jim Crow Childhood

> *It is a peculiar sensation, this double-consciousness, this sense of always looking at one's self through the eyes of others, of measuring one's soul by the tape of a world that looks on in amused contempt and pity. One ever feels his two-ness, - American, a Negro: two souls, two thoughts, two unreconciled strivings; two warring ideals in one dark body, whose dogged strength alone keeps it from being torn asunder.*
>
> —W. E. B. DuBois
> Author of *The Souls of Black Folk*

THELMA JEAN MOTHERSHED was born in Bloomburg, Texas, on November 29, 1940, to A. L. and Hosanna Claire Mothershed. They chose the name Thelma after Hosanna Claire's youngest sister. Thelma was the third child born after Lois and Grace, with whom she was close. Gilbert, the next child, was two and a half years younger than Thelma. Michael and Karen, born much later, rounded out the family.

A. L. and Hosanna Claire were model parents. She was a homemaker and gardener who prepared all of the meals and took care of the house. Hosanna Claire's children viewed her as a "jack of all trades." She also tended to the children when they were sick. A. L. was a devoted husband and father. He was regarded by his children as a very sincere, honest man who placed a high value on education. He always encouraged his children to reach for opportunities.[1]

A. L. was employed as a teacher at Bloomburg Academy—the school founded by his grandfather Oscar. During A. L.'s early career as a teacher, he was drafted into the army. While stationed at Texarkana, A. L.'s wife and daughters lived with his sister Leatha and her family.[2] A. L. was told he would probably be discharged and sent back to Bloomburg due to his responsibilities as a teacher and father of three. However, following the surprise attack at Pearl Harbor on December 7, 1941, America entered World War II and any hope of returning home was lost. A. L. was sent to Fort Leonard Wood in Missouri for training. He eventually reached the rank of second lieutenant. Thelma's earliest memory of her father came at age three when she and her mother waited at the train station to see him before he left for overseas duty.

While A. L. was away battling Hitler's forces in Europe, Hosanna Claire packed up the kids, left Bloomburg, and moved the family to Scott, Arkansas, in order that she might be closer to her own family. After the war, Thelma's family moved to North Little Rock in a neighborhood known as "Military Heights," which catered to many returning World War II veterans.[3] Upon his return, A. L. (or "Big AL" as the locals referred to him) got a job at the Fort Roots Veterans Administration Hospital while Hosanna Claire stayed home with the children. To supplement his income and provide for his family, A. L. took a second job as a waiter at Charlie Brown's Cowshed, a small café on Cantrell Road in North Little Rock. His son Gilbert was also employed there while in school, and the two actually worked together for a time.[4]

Summers were spent traveling to Bloomburg to visit Ollie Mae. The family took fresh water with them, as the well water on Ollie Mae's property was not potable. The children enjoyed these visits to see their grandmother and uncles on the farm. They especially liked Uncle B. F. (Benjamin Franklin) Mothershed, who had a knack for dealing with the temperamental animals on the farm.[5] Summertime was usually filled with great memories of relaxation and good food at Ollie Mae's farm. However, during the summer of 1946, young Thelma had a terrifying experience.

A. L. was taking Lois, Grace, Thelma, and Gilbert to visit their mother, who had contracted tuberculosis and was a patient at a sanatorium in Alexander, Arkansas. While on Roosevelt Road in front of the fairgrounds, the family encountered a policeman who raised his hand for A. L. to stop. A. L. complied,

A. L. Mothershed, circa 1940s. (Courtesy of Thelma Mothershed Wair)

Hosanna Claire Mothershed, circa 1940s. (Courtesy of Thelma Mothershed Wair)

but suddenly the car rolled a little. The tall, white, stern-looking officer stormed up to the vehicle. "Boy, didn't I tell you to stop!" he shouted. A. L. claimed the brakes had slipped accidently. The policeman then ordered A. L. out of the car, frightening young Thelma and her siblings.

The officer then put A. L. into the police car and drove the Mothershed's car farther down the street, parking it along the side of the road. The officer returned to his car and drove off with A. L., leaving Thelma and the others abandoned in the hot sun. Later, a white woman offered assistance, eventually taking them to their Aunt Mary's house. Mary was Hosanna Claire's sister in North Little Rock whom Thelma and her siblings lived with while their mother was in the sanatorium. A. L. returned later that night but remained silent about the events of that day. What was said or done to A. L. at police headquarters or how he was able to pick up the car would remain a mystery, for A. L. never spoke of the incident to the children again.[6]

***

As in the post-World War I era, blacks who returned from service in World War II were reluctant to return to Jim Crow segregation after fighting to defend liberty and freedom under the American flag. As a result of fighting abroad and experiencing wartime integration in defense industries on the home front, blacks now felt empowered to push for more rights. This was evident in national politics, as the number of northern black voters grew substantially.[7]

President Harry Truman recognized this electoral shift and thus appointed the Committee on Civil Rights whose job was to investigate racial discrimination and to offer suggestions on how best to address it. The committee issued a report entitled *To Secure These Rights* which proposed various civil rights measures which included anti-lynching and anti-poll tax legislation, eliminating segregation in interstate travel, and the establishment of a permanent civil rights commission.[8]

On February 2, 1948, President Truman stunned Americans when he delivered a special message to Congress in which he outlined his civil rights program, noting that "if we wish to fulfill the promise that is ours, we must correct the remaining imperfections in our practice of democracy." Truman designated civil rights as a Cold War issue, stressing the importance of democracy over the tenets of totalitarianism that was growing in Eastern Europe.[9] His remarks sent shockwaves among politicians in the Deep South, who felt the president was abandoning Democratic Party ideals. At the Democrats' annual Jefferson-Jackson Day celebration in mid-February, a speech by President Truman to mark the occasion was broadcast to several locations across the country. In Little Rock, Arkansas, over four hundred of the 850 party faithful who were crammed in a downtown hotel ballroom to hear the president's speech stormed out in protest.[10]

Truman's speech on civil rights was followed by an executive order to desegregate the armed forces. The desegregation of the defense industry during World War II had thrust the issue to the forefront. In 1946, the year after the German and Japanese surrender, the US Navy began integration. This was quickly followed by the newly re-organized air force. All eyes were on the US Army, which had a greater proportion of blacks than any of the other branches. Unwilling to wait on a slow Congress to enact legislation, President Truman issued Executive Order 9981 on July 26, 1948, which proclaimed that "there shall be equality of treatment and opportunity for all persons in the armed services without regard to race, color, religion, or national origin."[11] By the start of the Korean War in the summer of 1950, blacks and whites fought alongside one another in an integrated army.

It was an election year in 1948, and the president was running against Republican Governor Thomas Dewey of New York as well as opponents from within the Democratic Party. Truman's stance on civil rights and his executive order that desegregated the armed forces had caused so much anger among southern Democrats that they bolted from the party. The nomination of South Carolina Governor Strom Thurmond as the candidate for the segregationist States' Rights (or "Dixiecrat") Party soon followed.

That November, the election of Democratic Governor Sidney Sanders McMath symbolized a promising future for the state of Arkansas. McMath pledged reforms in healthcare, education, and welfare, along with economic advancement. To accomplish this, the state government would have to include blacks in this reform. President Truman lauded McMath's election, noting that Arkansas was "one of the most progressive states in the Union" and added "Arkansas stands on the threshold of a great opportunity."[12] Unfortunately, McMath and successive administrations failed to live up to that promise. While Arkansas witnessed some improvements in race relations during this period, including the admission of a black student to the University of Arkansas Law School and the desegregation of the public library, most public facilities remained segregated. Some "white" and "colored" signs were removed from drinking fountains, but segregation of restrooms was strictly enforced. While these reforms were significant, they did little to change the system of Jim Crow segregation. What little change that did occur during this period was a result of self-regulation by local whites rather than intervention on the part of the federal government.[13]

In the end, Truman won a narrow victory over Dewey. However, the Dixiecrat ticket of Thurmond and Fielding Wright garnered more than a million votes, its greatest strength coming from counties in the South which had the largest concentration of non-voting blacks.[14] The Democrats had regained control of Congress, restoring Southerners to powerful positions on congressional committees, and President Truman understood only too well that any further pursuance of his civil rights initiatives would not have support on Capitol Hill. After the onset of the Korean War and Senator Joseph McCarthy's attacks on communist subversion at home, talk of furthering civil rights quickly evaporated.[15] As increasing numbers of blacks fought segregation in the courts, it was clear if any reform in civil rights was to take place, it would have to come through the judicial rather than the executive branch.

***

For Thelma, her childhood was a difficult one. She was born a "blue baby" and tired very easily. Later, the family doctor told Hosanna Claire that her daughter had been born with tiny holes in her heart. Thelma would later learn this condition was known as "tetralogy of fallot," a type of congenital heart defect that results in low oxygen levels in the blood, thus giving the skin a bluish color during infancy. It can lead to poor development of the child, difficulty in gaining weight, and fainting spells. Because of this condition, doctors said Thelma would have trouble walking long distances, would not be able to run, and worst of all—she probably wouldn't live to see her sixteenth birthday. The news came as a crushing blow to A. L. and Hosanna Claire, and they decided to take the situation one day at a time.[16]

Thelma's physical limitations soon became apparent. One day while playing hopscotch, Thelma had to sit down because the activity was too much for her to endure. Walking with friends and family required frequent stops to rest, but the family found ways to cope with Thelma's illness. Lois and Grace frequently pulled Thelma in a small red wagon so she didn't have to walk. When her

Thelma Jean Mothershed, age two. (Courtesy of Thelma Mothershed Wair)

siblings and neighborhood children were playing baseball, Thelma would sit on the porch as a quiet observer. Once, the group let Thelma hit the ball while Grace ran the bases for her. On Sundays, the family traveled to Mt. Sinai Disciples of Christ Christian Church in North Little Rock.[17]

Attending movies also proved to be a challenge for Thelma. Jim Crow segregation dictated blacks be confined to movie theater balconies, but Thelma couldn't climb stairs without difficulty. Instead, Thelma opted to go to the GEM Theatre on Saturdays with her brother Gilbert. The GEM was the all-black movie theater and only showed old movies, but that didn't stop Thelma and Gilbert from enjoying the time together.[18] Over the course of time, Thelma learned to accept her physical limitations.

It was during this time Thelma also learned the limitations of her race. Once, while traveling to Ollie Mae's farm in Bloomburg, the family stopped at a gas station for Thelma to use the restroom. She was shocked when told by the attendant she was not allowed to use it. Afterwards, her parents explained to her that she was denied the use of the restroom because of her color. Soon after, on a trip to downtown Little Rock's department stores, she noticed drinking fountains and restrooms with "White Only" signs above them. Jim Crow segregation outlined a pattern of social interaction between the races that both whites and blacks understood and were expected to abide. Whenever she questioned it, the answer was, "That's just the way things are." It was a statement young Thelma would never forget.[19]

Thelma's elementary education began at Hillside School in North Little Rock, where she attended first and second grade. For third through fifth grade, she was homeschooled in North Little Rock. Her home study teacher, Bernice Wright, instructed her in the basics for an hour each day. During her fifth-grade year, the family moved to Little Rock, and Thelma continued to be homeschooled. However, for the sixth grade, Thelma actually attended Bush Elementary School in Little Rock. An arrangement was made with the administration allowing Thelma to use the portable classrooms that had been set up for special education students. Thelma was one of twelve students in the makeshift classroom and sat in the corner working in an independent study fashion, longing to be in a regular classroom setting.[20]

Once Thelma reached the seventh grade, she attended Dunbar Jr./Sr. High School in Little Rock. By this time, the Mothersheds had moved to a house at 1313 Chester Street in Little Rock and Dunbar (located on 15th Street and Wright Avenue) was only a few blocks away. Paul Lawrence Dunbar High School was built in 1929, serving grades seven through twelve as well as housing Dunbar Junior College, a training center for black teachers. Dunbar was the only accredited secondary school for blacks in Arkansas. It offered a wide variety of classes and earned a reputation as being "the best-equipped black school" in the United States.[21] Even when the family lived in North Little Rock, A. L. and Hosanna Claire knew the value of Dunbar and sent both Lois and Grace to the school. Thelma would follow in her sisters' footsteps. In an era before handicapped accessibility, Thelma's counselors were very accommodating and scheduled all of her classes on the main level at Dunbar.[22]

It was there Thelma met and became close friends with Minnijean Brown and Melba Patillo. Minnijean was a very outgoing, energetic young girl who had a zest for life and all it had to offer. Melba was an elegant, fashion-conscious teen who knew proper etiquette and relished her role as leader of all things social. Often, Thelma, Melba, and Minnie would drive around in Minnie's mother's car and hang out or go to Gilliam Park, the all-black swimming pool located on Little Rock's east side. Of course, her condition prevented Thelma from swimming, so she would just put her feet in the water and enjoy watching Minnie and Melba swim. The three girls formed a tight-knit relationship and later constituted a third of the students who would integrate Central High School in 1957.

Life at Dunbar was good for Thelma as she was thrilled to finally be a part of a regular classroom setting. She made friends easily and her peers readily accepted her physical limitations. If it didn't bother her, then it didn't bother them. She focused on her studies and throughout her three years at Dunbar, Thelma excelled academically. In eighth grade, she was inducted into the Junior High National Honor Society, and the following year she served as the organization's president.[23]

For the present, Thelma focused on poodle skirts, the latest rock-n-roll songs, and just enjoying life as a teenager. As the country braced itself for one of the most important Supreme Court cases of the twentieth century, Thelma and her friends had no idea what impact the *Brown v. Board of Education* case would have on race relations in America or of their role as major players in the movement that lay ahead.

CHAPTER 2
Setting the Stage: *Brown v. Board*

Does segregation of children in public schools solely on the basis of race, even though the physical facilities and other "tangible" factors may be equal, deprive the children of the minority group of equal educational opportunities? We believe that it does.

—Earl Warren
Fourteenth chief justice of the United States (1954–1969)

IN THE LONG HISTORY of the Supreme Court, a few cases have rocked America to its core. So it was when the ruling on the infamous *Brown v. Board of Education* case was handed down on Monday, May 17, 1954. Chief Justice Earl Warren, a liberal newcomer to the high court appointed by President Eisenhower to replace the recently deceased Fred Vinson, stated unequivocally that "in the field of public education the doctrine of 'separate but equal' has no place."[1] With the stroke of the pen, the highest court struck down over fifty years of de jure segregation in public educational facilities.

In 1896, the court had effectively legalized segregation through its ruling in *Plessy v. Ferguson*. Up to that point, segregation was the unwritten law of the land, established in the North as well as the South as a means of control over former slaves during Reconstruction. When a black man by the name of Homer Plessy was arrested in Louisiana, his subsequent trial became national news and changed the nature of race relations in the United States for the next six decades.

In a carefully orchestrated and choreographed moment, Homer Plessy refused to ride in the separate "Jim Crow" car set aside for blacks on the East Louisiana Railroad. Plessy, who was one-eighth black, could effectively pass for being white and purposefully sat in the white car, testing the recent Separate Car

Act passed by the State of Louisiana in 1890.[2] Plessy was arrested and when his case reached Washington, the Supreme Court drew the color line in the sand, stating that "if one race be inferior to the other socially, the constitution of the United States cannot put them on the same plane."[3] The Supreme Court had now defined the clear distinctions between the races and "separate but equal" became the law of the land.

In the years following the *Plessy* case, black organizations, particularly the National Association for the Advancement of Colored People (NAACP), worked hard at erasing the decision from 1896. It wasn't until the early Cold War period of the 1940s–1950s that their attempts to integrate society would pay off. Executive orders by Presidents Roosevelt and Truman integrated defense industries during World War II and the armed forces, respectively. American society was on the verge of change. In the *Sweatt v. Painter* ruling of June 25, 1950, the court struck down segregation in law schools and allowed blacks entry into those institutions.[4] This was followed on the very same day with another ruling, *McLaurin v. Oklahoma State Regents*, which opened up the doors of white graduate schools for blacks.[5] Even though the Supreme Court stopped short of overturning *Plessy* on those two occasions, it was evident the times were indeed changing. The biggest change, however, would come from an unlikely place in the United States—Topeka, Kansas.

Like most cities in the country, Topeka in the 1950s was a divided city—there were both all-white and all-black schools, which had been racially segregated for decades. One of Topeka's black residents, Oliver Brown, was a minister whose seven-year-old daughter Linda attended an all-black school. Despite living in close proximity to an all-white school, Linda had to walk several blocks, cross a busy railroad switchyard, and catch a run-down bus to attend her school five miles away. The NAACP seized upon this opportunity to focus their next attack on legalized segregation.[6]

As in the *Sweatt* and *McLaurin* cases, the NAACP strategy in the *Brown* case was a simple two-pronged approach. Separate educational facilities, they said, denied equal educational opportunity because the all-black schools lacked the advantages of traditional all-white schools. Secondly, the NAACP focused on the psychological damage inflicted on blacks due to segregation, which created a mindset that blacks were somehow inferior to whites.[7]

To head up this monumental task of convincing the court that segregation was wrong, the NAACP chose its top lawyer, Thurgood Marshall. A grandson of slaves himself, Marshall rose in prominence to become the NAACP's top legal strategist and revered civil rights lawyer. Marshall's plan was to show the court that "separate but equal" was a myth, as damaging to the perpetrators as it was to the recipients. His defense included expert testimony from school administrators showing the discrepancies between all-black and all-white schools in everything from curricula to facilities. His most important evidence, however, came from psychologists and sociologists, who pointed out the negative effects segregation had upon black children's emotional and intellectual abilities when compared to white children of the same age.

At the time of Chief Justice Vinson's sudden death, the court remained divided on the *Brown* case. Only after some persuading by incoming Chief Justice Earl Warren did the court hand down a unanimous verdict. Carefully written, the *Brown* ruling did not declare the US Constitution to be colorblind, nor did it condemn the reasoning behind the *Plessy* case some fifty-eight years prior. Instead, the court based their decision upon psychological factors that a segregated education was "inherently" unequal, causing emotional harm and slowing mental development of black schoolchildren.[8]

Reactions to the *Brown* ruling were mixed. For conservative Southerners, the ruling was an outrage. The next day, southern newspapers were filled with editorials denouncing the decision. The *Daily News* from Jackson, Mississippi, stated, "White and Negro children in the same schools will lead to miscegenation. Miscegenation leads to mixed marriages and mixed marriages lead to the mongrelization of the human race."[9] By contrast, the *Chicago Defender*, a black-run newspaper, recognized the handwriting on the wall. "Neither the atom bomb nor the hydrogen bomb will ever be as meaningful to our democracy as the unanimous declaration of the Supreme Court that racial segregation violates the spirit and the letter of our Constitution," it rejoiced. "This means the beginning of the end of the dual society in American life and the . . . segregation which supported it."[10] Others, like the *Arkansas Gazette*, took a more moderate view, stating, "The new patterns will have to be hammered out across the table in thousands of scattered school districts, and they will have to be shaped to accommodate not only the needs but the prejudices of whites and Negroes to whom these problems are not abstractions but the essence of their daily lives."[11]

For as monumental as the *Brown* case was, it still had not wiped out segregation across America. By the mid-1950s, Congress had not passed any laws against segregation in public places. Still, it was unsettling as to how far this case would actually go in changing the nature of race relations in America. All eyes were on the man whose opinion would matter most in this case—President Dwight D. Eisenhower.

A moderate on the issue of civil rights, Eisenhower later said the biggest mistake of his presidency was appointing Warren as chief justice.[12] The appointment was a political favor for former California governor Warren, who campaigned for Ike in his home state during the election of 1952. The president now found himself in an awkward position. After the court's ruling, Eisenhower was asked to take steps to help ease the transformation and make the adjustment a peaceful one. These included calling a national conference of both southern white and black moderates, a speaking tour of the South drumming up support and respect for the Supreme Court, and utilizing the new medium of television to appeal to citizens for their understanding and patience regarding these matters. However, the president did none of these things. When asked in a press conference whether or not he endorsed the recent ruling, Eisenhower cautiously replied he did not think it mattered whether or not he endorsed it, just that he must conform to it.[13]

Resistance in the South intensified, and just weeks after the *Brown* decision, the first White Citizens' Council was formed in Indianola, Mississippi, and quickly spread to neighboring states, including Arkansas. The White Citizens' Councils attracted political and economic elites among the South and chose to use segregationist speeches and propaganda rather than the noose of the ghostly robed Ku Klux Klansmen to get their points across.[14] What began as a campaign to mount resistance against the Supreme Court's integration decree soon took on a new form of racism. The White Citizens' Councils' handbook, *Black Monday* (referring to the day of the *Brown* ruling) written by segregationist Mississippi Judge Thomas Brady, spoke of the dangers of race mixing. This was followed by numerous other council publications that warned Southerners that little white girls could contract syphilis from the "drinking fountains, books, towels, and gym clothes" used by the black students.[15] As the controllers of economic interests, White Citizen' Councils could inflict hardship through boycotts of local black businesses, denial of credit to black customers, and unemployment among sharecroppers in their areas. Membership of these councils quickly swelled into the hundreds of thousands in the months that followed.[16]

Knowing that adherence to the *Brown* decision would be difficult for the states to accept, Chief Justice Warren devised a "remedy" phase known as *Brown II*, which took nearly a year of the court's time in deliberations. In this ruling, the chief justice offered relief to states affected by the initial *Brown* ruling, citing various local conditions that needed to be handled by the federal district courts, while at the same time prompting local school districts to comply with the decision. On May 31, 1955, Warren said, "The courts may consider problems related to administration, arising from the physical condition of the plant, the school transportation system, personnel, revision of school districts and attendance areas into compact units to achieve a system of determining admission to the public schools on a non-racial basis, and revision of local laws and regulations which may be necessary in solving the foregoing problems." He further urged school districts comply "with all deliberate speed."[17]

Southern communities reacted with horror. To them, their way of life was being shattered by the high court, and some states made it abundantly clear they would refuse to accept the ruling. As with other controversial rulings, the Supreme Court provided no answer to the difficult questions of what constituted impermissible segregation, timetables for compliance, or the proper steps to achieve racial balance in the public schools in the least threatening way.[18] Those decisions, the court thought, were best handled by the local courts and individual school boards.

One of the first places those tough decisions were made occurred in 1955 in the little town of Hoxie. A delta town in northeastern Arkansas, Hoxie had 1,855 residents and opened school in July in order to allow farm children to have cotton-picking time off during the autumn months. *LIFE* magazine reported that while other southern communities were "looking for loopholes" in the *Brown* ruling, Hoxie's school board talked to parents in its community and determined the time was right to comply, calling the decision to integrate "morally right in the sight of God."[19]

While Hoxie's integration was not the first in Arkansas, it was still met with mixed feelings from its residents. Its location in the eastern part of the state meant the racial pattern was different than in western Arkansas where previous school integration had taken place at Fayetteville and Charleston in the autumn of 1954. Eastern Arkansas was known for its cotton production and sharecropping, with segregation being much more deeply rooted.[20] Some angry whites had threatened a boycott of the school, while others simply voiced their dissatisfaction with the new arrangement. The first integrated school day started tense with an unusually quiet bus ride in which some white students chose to stand in the aisle rather than sit next to the new black students. On that first day, twenty-one black children arrived at the school and no violence erupted.[21] Throughout the day, teachers accommodated the new pupils while anxious parents looked on. However, *LIFE* reported that by the noon recess, the boys and girls, both white and black, happily played together and by the end of the day behaved "as if they had gone to school together all their lives."[22]

Meanwhile, those in positions of power in the southern states continued trying to nullify the *Brown* ruling and prevent further incidents like the one in Hoxie. To express their outrage at the decision, on March 12, 1956, 101 of the 128 members of Congress representing the southern states issued the "Declaration of Constitutional Principles." More commonly known as "The Southern Manifesto," this document condemned the Supreme Court for overreaching its bounds, abusing its power, and encroaching on the rights of the states.[23] The US Constitution, they argued, did not mention education; therefore, it should be left up to states sovereignty. They further reinforced that the interpretation of "separate but equal" outlined in the *Plessy* decision had become a part of the habits and customs of those living in the South, both white and black, and called the actions by the Supreme Court in *Brown* and *Brown II* as an "unwarranted exercise of power by the court."[24] They blamed the court for creating chaos and confusion among the southern states, which threatened to break down race relations in the South, and warned the public education system in some states was in danger of being destroyed.

What followed was a frenzy of debates from statehouses to coffee shops. The White Citizens' Councils began an elaborate propaganda campaign indicating they favored closing public schools rather than integrating them. Terms such as "states' rights" and "nullification," not heard in nearly a hundred years, became part of the national discourse as the country braced itself for a new kind of civil war. Senator Harry F. Byrd, from the usually moderate state of Virginia, led the rallying cries of "interposition" and "massive resistance" and encouraged his southern neighbors to adopt a private school plan which would evade the court's decision.[25] Membership in the Ku Klux Klan surged during this period, as the organization employed its usual tactics of intimidation and terror while defending the principles of segregation and white supremacy.

Progress towards compliance with the Supreme Court's ruling was very slow, occurring mainly in the border states and upper- to mid-southern states such as Arkansas. When the 1956–1957 school year began, only 723 school districts desegregated across the South, with some three thousand remaining in a segregated state.[26] Despite small gains in Tennessee, Texas, and Arkansas, some 2.4 million black pupils were denied the right to a better education.[27] If change was going to come, it would have to be through a grand spectacle that no one, not even the president of the United States, could ignore. Arkansas would once again be the center of attention, this time at Little Rock Central High School.

CHAPTER 3
The Blossom Plan

It is unlikely that ever again in this struggle over civil rights will there be a more clear-cut issue of respect for and obedience to the law, or that organized propaganda, economic pressures, and selfish political scheming will again be so artfully combined to turn the optimum situation into a national disaster.

—Virgil T. Blossom
Superintendent of Little Rock Schools (1953–1958)

CLOSE TO FIVE-THOUSAND people attended Central High School's dedication after its completion in the spring of 1927. The mammoth building stood like a cathedral encompassing two city blocks on Park Avenue between 14th and 16th Streets. Visitors marveled at its architecture. Its new letterhead even referred to the structure as "the most beautiful high school in America." Four statues, titled *Ambition, Personality, Opportunity,* and *Preparation,* stood like silent caretakers over the tri-arched doorway. Thirty years later, that entrance would grace the cover of every major newspaper and magazine around the world as integration took place. For the moment, though, Central was for whites only. "Built like a fortress," author David Margolick remarked, "it proved impregnable to Little Rock's black children. Its manicured grounds might just as well have been a moat."[1] Black students at Dunbar High School could only dream of what opportunities might lay before them if they had a chance to attend Central. Their current textbooks were hand-me downs from Central, and many opened them only to find racial epithets written inside—a daily, painful reminder of the two worlds they lived in.

Just five days after the initial *Brown* ruling, the Little Rock School Board met and agreed to comply with the Supreme Court's desegregation order pending further instructions.² Working closely with the school board was Virgil Blossom, superintendent of the Little Rock School District. A big, burly man of intense stature, Blossom commanded attention whenever he entered a room. His thick, horn-rimmed glasses exuded an appearance of old-school authority. Blossom's niece, author Elizabeth Jacoway, described him as "earnest, businesslike, and serious" who "tended to dramatize or magnify things that concerned him."³ Upon learning of the school board's decision, Blossom instructed his staff to research the matter. He was the featured speaker at numerous community meetings and informally polled hundreds of local residents from all walks of life about their views on integration.⁴

Blossom focused on five important points as he spoke to the civic leadership of Little Rock. This involved: (1) calling for each school district to develop its own plan for integration tailored to its own conditions, (2) approaching the problem from an intelligent viewpoint and not an emotional one, (3) emphasizing respect for the law, (4) respecting the rights of everyone involved, and (5) maintaining educational standards while cooperating with local black residents in an orderly plan of integration.⁵ Initially, Blossom favored integrating Little Rock schools at the elementary level. "It seemed to me that six year-old children would be the least concerned about the color of the skin of classmates," he later wrote. "They would not have had time to develop strong prejudices or to become traditionalists."⁶ However, when the "Blossom Plan" was revealed on May 24, 1955, it contained a very different approach.

The plan called for desegregation beginning only at the high school level with a small, carefully screened group of black applicants. Based on their research, Blossom and the school board concluded it would be a great mistake to start integration at the elementary level because in some schools (particularly the eastern ones), blacks outnumbered whites by a ratio of almost fifty to one. Additionally, Superintendent Blossom claimed that as he conversed with parents of younger children, he found them to be more vehemently opposed to integration than parents of older students. Beginning integration at the high school level, Blossom believed, would lessen its impact, as fewer students and teachers would be affected.⁷

Implementation of the Blossom Plan was slated for the fall of 1957 after construction was completed on two new high schools—Horace Mann and Hall High. The latter was to be built in the northwest part of the city and thus cater to the all-white, affluent suburbs. Horace Mann, located in the eastern part of the city where the population was predominantly black, was to replace Dunbar, which was overcrowded, outdated, and in need of repair. Furthermore, the school board hired an all-black staff for Horace Mann and stated it would open as an all-black school in 1956. The fact blacks were getting a new school was perceived by some that the school board was only doing this in the hopes of forestalling integration.

In response to the Blossom Plan, neighboring cities of North Little Rock, Fort Smith, and Hot Springs decided to delay any further integration action until the capital city made its move.[8] To black leaders and the NAACP, this abrupt change in Blossom's original plan to integrate all schools in Little Rock seemed as though he was bowing to the segregationists' demands by focusing on just one high school—Central High. Therefore, Central was left to bear the burden of integration, so the administration began preparations for the upcoming transition.

Central's Faculty Guidance Committee decided to hold a series of assemblies to prepare the students for the upcoming integration.[9] Assisting the committee was the girls' vice principal, Elizabeth Huckaby. Huckaby heard Dr. Hugh Brown of the Arkansas State Tuberculosis Sanatorium for Negroes speak at a recent meeting of social workers and invited him to be a part of a panel discussion on integration at Central. This panel consisted of doctors, educators, and social service coordinators as well as students.[10] During the presentation, only one vocalized comment from a faculty member and one written question from a student (not included in the Q & A) inquired as to why a black person was included on the panel. Otherwise, the assembly ended without incident. Considering the crowd numbered around two thousand, the committee felt as if the process of educating the students about integration was successful.[11]

Things were progressing according to plan when Jess Matthews, Central's principal, informed Miss Huckaby that Superintendent Blossom had a different approach. To Miss Huckaby's surprise, Blossom instructed that high school committees were not to take part in any community preparation for the integration of Central. Instead, he would take care of it himself by appearing before civic organizations and informing them of the process.[12] The absence of school leadership in such a monumental undertaking left some faculty members and administrators at Central feeling betrayed by Blossom. Suspicions abounded that Blossom was backtracking to appeal to segregationist parents and political leaders.

To make matters worse, local officials offered no assistance as Little Rock's government was in the midst of changing to a city manager style of administration. Woodrow Mann, the lame-duck mayor, lacked power to enforce any new policy, often arguing with city council members and weakening local leadership.[13] The Right Reverend Robert R. Brown, Episcopal bishop of the Diocese of Little Rock, condemned city leaders for not helping the public ease into this transition. "There was no board or committee with the formal authority to advise, educate, or assist other city leaders in preparing comprehensively for desegregation."[14] Instead, city officials left the task of finding a solution up to the school board.

Superintendent Blossom's methods aroused the ire of Daisy Bates, the strong-willed leader of the Arkansas branch of the NAACP and the wife of L. C. Bates, owner of the *Arkansas State Press*, a black publication. In an effort to speed up the integration process, Mrs. Bates decided to make a legal test of Blossom's plan. She perceived it to be an empty promise that would drag out the integration issue indefinitely. On the morning of January 24, 1956, Mrs. Bates and a group of black students ranging from first grade to high school arrived in the superintendent's office demanding they be allowed to register in all grades for the second semester. Blossom refused, stating he was going to follow the board's plan of gradual integration.[15]

Two weeks later, Wiley Branton, state chairman of the NAACP's Legal Defense Committee, and U. Simpson Tate, regional NAACP attorney, filed suit against the Little Rock School District in federal court calling for immediate integration.[16] The court upheld the school board's plan and the NAACP appealed the decision. The court of appeals upheld the lower court, however, and ordered the Little Rock School Board to begin integrating in the fall of 1957 under the supervision of the federal district court. Even though Daisy Bates and the NAACP didn't receive the immediate integration they originally fought for, it was clear integration would finally take place under federal court jurisdiction.[17]

Meanwhile, Central made preparations to become an integrated school. On March 27, 1957, at 7:30 pm, Central hosted its annual "Ninth Grade Night." This open house allowed ninth graders (who were soon to enter Central) and their parents to hear from the principal and students about extracurricular activities the high school had to offer. Only students from the white junior high schools were invited to attend this meeting. Principal Matthews asked Superintendent Blossom to speak to the assembled parents and students about the desegregation of Central in the fall. To everyone's surprise, Blossom sat down after delivering brief welcoming remarks. He neither discussed the upcoming change nor answered any questions regarding it.[18]

***

Thelma was a sophomore during the 1956–1957 school year. Since Dunbar was now a junior high school, Thelma attended the brand new Horace Mann. Despite the fact Thelma lived within the boundaries of Central High's school district, she had to ride the city bus to school. Thelma would walk a block and a quarter to the 15th Street bus stop. A bus would pick Thelma up and take her to the stop at 14th and Main Streets. Here, she would switch to another bus that would take her to 25th Street (also known as Roosevelt Road) by Horace Mann. The fare was five cents one way.[19]

In May of 1957, the Little Rock School Board sent a letter to the students at Horace Mann, requesting volunteers for the upcoming integration at Central. Dr. Leroy Christophe, principal of Horace Mann, called an assembly to inform the students that Central was planning to integrate and they would have the opportunity to attend classes there beginning in the fall. Over two-hundred students signed up to transfer, including Thelma. Despite advances at Horace Mann, Central offered more classes, used newer textbooks, had more clubs, and best of all—afforded chances for college scholarships. Thelma's family never doubted she was destined to continue her education past high school. Thelma's sisters Lois and Grace had already paved the way. After attending Dunbar, Lois entered Phillips University (as their first black student) in 1955 and Grace continued her education while majoring in nursing at the University of Arkansas. Thelma wanted to go into teaching after high school and attending Central could make that dream come true. After all, Thelma thought, why shouldn't she be allowed to go to a school for which her parents pay taxes anyway?[20]

That afternoon, Thelma shared the news with her mother that she had signed up to transfer to Central. As Thelma got into the car at the bus stop, she showed her the form. "Are you stupid?" Hosanna Claire anxiously inquired. "Don't you know how big that school is? How are you going to manage all of those stairs?" Hosanna Claire thought it best to table the discussion until A. L. came home. That evening, Thelma convinced her parents she was sure the counselors at Central would accommodate her as they had at Dunbar and that she was up for the challenge. Central was in their neighborhood, Thelma stated, so she wouldn't have to take the bus, thus saving the family money. Besides, her friends Minnijean Brown and Melba Patillo had decided to transfer there as well. A. L. and Hosanna Claire, while privately reserved, supported their daughter's decision to enter Central that fall and signed the transfer form.[21]

Daisy Bates had contacted all of the black students who were interested in attending Central that fall and arranged a meeting between them and Superintendent Blossom. Blossom knew that admitting all two-hundred-plus students would be a scheduling nightmare and would disrupt classes. The addition of that many blacks to the student body would no doubt inflame members of the segregationist community. Therefore, he told the students to keep a "low profile – go to school and then go home."[22] In addition, students who wanted to transfer were told they couldn't participate in extracurricular activities. This disappointed Thelma, who hoped to be a part of the National Honor Society as she had been president at Dunbar. Minnijean wanted to sing in the choir and was told she could not. Participation in sports was definitely out of the question as administrators feared rival schools would boycott games with Central if black students were allowed to play. After meeting with Superintendent Blossom, two-thirds of the students decided they didn't want to transfer after all. Mrs. Bates became even more convinced Blossom was trying to hurt the integration process while claiming he supported it.[23]

As a result of this meeting, seventeen students were chosen to enroll based on their mental ability, scholastic achievement, citizenship records, and deportment. Eight of them backed out by the time school started in September of 1957. Grateful for the opportunity to receive a quality education, the remaining students rose to the challenge and chose to leave Horace Mann and their comfort zone behind. They were Thelma and her friends Minnijean and Melba, along with Elizabeth Eckford, Carlotta Walls, Gloria Ray, Jefferson Thomas, Terrence Roberts, and Ernest Green. Together, they would be thrust into the national spotlight as the "Little Rock Nine."

CHAPTER 4
Opposition Mounts

I will not force my people to integrate against their will. I will fight to preserve the rights guaranteed to the people, and that includes control of the school.

—Orval Faubus
Thirty-sixth governor of Arkansas (1955–1967)

AS NEWS OF THE BLOSSOM PLAN filtered through the public, segregationists in Little Rock began voicing their dissatisfaction. This, in turn, sparked hostility among middle-class whites in Little Rock, creating resentment against those affluent whites whose children would not have to attend an integrated school. Central High School was positioned adjacent to the white working-class and black neighborhoods. According to author Wilmer Counts, "The old working-class neighborhoods would bear the stresses of the social experiment of school integration, while the affluent white preserves would enjoy pristine white schools that would be spared the strains of educating children of both races in the same classrooms."[1] The fault lines in Little Rock had been set—residents were just as much divided over class as they were race. Some in the capital city lay the blame for this tension at the feet of the federal government, some at the feet of Virgil Blossom, and for many others, blame rested with Arkansas Governor Orval Faubus.

Orval Faubus was elected governor of Arkansas in 1954, the same year as the historic *Brown* case. From the outset, Faubus was the kind of politician who could read not only public opinion but also the needs and wants of legislators.[2] As governor, he often worked eighteen hours a day. He responded to every letter that came across his desk and loved being in the limelight, traveling the state giving speeches and attending ribbon-cutting ceremonies.[3] As far as integration was concerned, Faubus made few remarks about it. In his first term as governor, several Arkansas school districts, including Hoxie, had integrated successfully. However, by the time of his campaign for re-election, Faubus knew he would have to take a stand on the issue. Because Arkansas law required a governor serve only a two-year term, Faubus was constantly looking towards the next election. He realized early in 1956 that if he did not come out as a strong opponent of the Blossom Plan, he would risk losing his bid for re-election. His main challenger was a young politician named Jim Johnson. Johnson had led a campaign in 1954 to amend the Arkansas state constitution in the hopes of circumventing the orders of the Supreme Court's ruling in the *Brown* decision.[4] Now, Johnson was challenging Faubus in the gubernatorial primary of 1956. Faubus was particularly concerned about losing support in the southeastern part of the state known as the Delta. This region was dominated by white cotton plantation owners who relied heavily on black labor. Johnson's popularity was quickly growing in the Delta, and Faubus understood he could no longer afford to stay on the sidelines when it came to the issue of segregation.

It had been rumored Faubus could be a possible contender for the vice presidency with Adlai Stevenson in the fall of 1956 and he did not want to make waves which could damage his political ambitions.[5] As a result, Faubus took the path of moderation, choosing to sit back and see how other states dealt with the issue of integration. Hard-line segregationists both in and out of Arkansas took notice and condemned Faubus for his stance. Some of the harshest criticism against Faubus came from Mississippi Senator James O. Eastland. In one fiery speech at Tupelo, Mississippi, Senator Eastland warned, "There is now being waged a tremendous conflict in the border states, which will determine what will happen to the Deep South. If the Southern states are picked off one by one under the damnable doctrine of gradualism I don't know if we can hold out or not."[6]

Faubus carefully danced around the issue of integration and played up his support for whatever side he addressed on the campaign trail. He told his audience exactly what they wanted to hear, often contradicting himself. In one campaign speech in Pine Bluff, Arkansas, the governor began with a statement assuring the crowd that segregation was not an issue in the campaign. After this remark brought a wave of boos and jeers from the audience, the governor concluded in the same sentence that he would uphold the state's traditional stance on segregation.[7] The audience then cheered loudly.

Even though few Arkansans understood exactly where the governor stood on the issue of integration, he easily defeated Johnson for a second term. Hoping the issue was behind him, Faubus settled into the task of setting the agenda for his second administration. A liberal who supported socially progressive programs, Faubus was mindful of the support needed from eastern conservative politicians to enact such measures as tax increases to cover education and welfare programs.[8] These same eastern politicians were also the driving force behind halting integration in Arkansas. As a result, Faubus threw his support behind four anti-integration bills passed in the spring of 1957. These created a State Sovereignty Commission, removed compulsory attendance requirements for integrated schools, required groups like the NAACP to register financial records with the state, and allowed school boards the use of funds to hire lawyers for integration suits.[9]

Meanwhile in Little Rock, Virgil Blossom was finding it necessary to defend his plan for integration. Newspaper editorials across the Deep South attacked the superintendent as a "carpetbagger" from Missouri and as a disciple of the NAACP. As the summer of 1957 progressed, advertisements and leaflets were sent to parents of white students calling the integration plan one of "race-mixing" and encouraged them to withdraw their children from Central.[10] Blossom, concerned for the safety of his students, tried on numerous occasions to persuade Governor Faubus to publicly state there was to be no violence or disorder when school began. According to Blossom, Faubus refused because he feared such a statement would be misinterpreted as one in support of integration.[11] The governor had maneuvered himself into a political corner and his silence on the matter only intensified the segregationists' efforts. All of this was changed after a visit to Little Rock from Georgia Governor Marvin Griffin.

At the behest of Jim Johnson and as a ploy to put more pressure on Faubus, Marvin Griffin was invited to Little Rock on August 22, 1957. The Georgia governor was to be the keynote speaker at the Hotel Marion for a $10-a-plate dinner hosted by the Capital Citizens' Council. When Faubus heard Griffin was coming, he called and asked him not to come as the situation in Little Rock was getting "tense." After being assured by Griffin that there would be no problem, Faubus reluctantly allowed Griffin to stay at the governor's mansion while in Little Rock, worrying how integrationists would view this visit.[12]

Before a crowd of 350, whom he praised as "courageous patriots," Griffin proudly defended Georgia's record in maintaining segregation and encouraged the citizens of Little Rock to oppose the Blossom Plan as well as the Supreme Court order to desegregate schools. He called upon Governor Faubus to do the same. Griffin defiantly stated that if the federal government threatened to withhold funding for school lunch programs if Georgia didn't comply with the court order, he would tell them to "take their black-eyed peas and soup pots out of Georgia." His remarks earned him a standing ovation from the audience. As the crowd left the hotel ballroom, they asked themselves—if Georgia is so brave in standing up to the federal government and resisting integration, why not Arkansas?[13]

That same evening, around 11:00 pm, Daisy Bates had just come inside after taking her dog out for a walk when suddenly a rock came crashing through the living room window. L. C. rushed into the room to find his wife on the floor covered in glass. As she got up, Mrs. Bates saw a note tied to the rock with the words, "STONE THIS TIME. DYNAMITE NEXT."[14] A few days later, Daisy and her husband awoke to a find a burning cross on their front lawn with a sign that read, "Go back to Africa – KKK."[15]

As September approached, the Capital Citizens' Council ramped up its efforts to halt integration. About half of the organization's five-hundred members lived outside Little Rock, yet they were very vocal about the impact the upcoming desegregation of Central would have at both the state and local level.[16] Governor Faubus's office was being inundated with letters, telegrams, and telephone calls asking the governor to speak out against the impending integration of Central High.

Another factor that led to increased tension in the weeks leading up to the desegregation of Central was the formation of the Mothers' League. The Mothers' League was a pro-segregationist organization made up of working-class women of the Little Rock community, many of whom had children that attended Central. The group was formed in August 1957 and was devoted to the prevention of violence as well as rejecting the integration of Central High School.[17] What started out as a small group of women ballooned after Governor Griffin's speech. The group's first meeting took place at the home of Mrs. Clyde A. Thomason with thirty-nine in attendance (nine of whom were male members of the Capital Citizens' Council). Soon, the women stepped up their efforts, recruiting members via a phone tree. One dedicated mother made around two-hundred calls. The next meeting was held at the Lafayette Hotel and drew a crowd of several hundred ladies.[18] In addition to mounting an intense propaganda campaign, the group also circulated a petition to oust Superintendent Blossom and all integrationists on the school board.

The Mothers' League feared miscegenation and worried the admission of the nine Negro students would threaten their white heritage. This belief was rooted in the misguided notion that race mixing would naturally result from blacks and whites inhabiting the same classrooms. In her dissertation, Phoebe Godfrey concluded, "For poor and working-class whites, like those in the Mothers' League, integration was a direct threat to privileges based on whiteness. Anti-miscegenation laws, both on the books and based on folk-ways, gave poor and working-class whites a legally and socially enforced way to ensure 'white grandchildren.'"[19] As a combined force of determined women, the Mothers' League was very effective in putting pressure on Governor Faubus to halt the integration.

On August 27, five days after Governor Griffin's speech and the rock incident at the Bates' house, Mrs. Thomason of the Mothers' League filed a suit in Pulaski County Chancery Court seeking an injunction to halt school integration.[20] The suit was heard two days later, with Governor Faubus testifying. Both he and Mrs. Thomason (without revealing their sources) claimed both whites and Negroes were arming themselves with guns and knives.[21] When asked about the governor's testimony, Little Rock Police Chief Marvin Potts said, "Let's say that I haven't heard what Governor Faubus says he has heard."[22] Faubus concluded by saying now was not a good time for Central to integrate. Judge Murray Reed agreed and granted the injunction. That night, segregationists drove by the Bates' house, honking their horns and yelling, "Daisy! Daisy! Did you hear the news? The coons won't be going to Central!"[23]

The next day, NAACP attorneys Wiley Branton and Thurgood Marshall filed a petition to seek nullification of the injunction, and Judge Ronald Davies agreed. The desegregation of Central High School could proceed as planned. Central High School Vice Principal Elizabeth Huckaby, along with most of the faculty, wondered what the new school year would hold. She wrote in her journal, "Federal Court in no uncertain terms ordered integration for Tuesday and enjoined all interference. Made the situation clearer, more stable." She looked forward to a peaceful transition to the start of school.[24]

On Saturday, August 31, just three days before the start of school, Superintendent Blossom received a late-night phone call. It was Governor Faubus and he wanted Blossom to come to the governor's mansion immediately. On a hot, steamy night the two men sat up for three hours discussing the impending integration. Blossom did most of the talking as Faubus, while pleasant and attentive, appeared at times to be vague in his agreement to proceed with the integration. At one point, Blossom felt he had convinced the governor to make a statement in support of the school board, but then the mood turned somber. The long night concluded with Faubus telling Blossom, "I'll call you when I decide . . . but I don't think I'm going to let you do it."[25]

Monday, September 2, 1957, was Labor Day. School was to start at Central the next day. At 9:00 pm, Blossom, who was in an emergency meeting with his school board, received a telephone call informing him that National Guardsmen had surrounded Central High School and the governor was going to make a televised speech at 10:15 pm.[26] Faubus began his speech touting Arkansas's impressive record on race relations. He cited the various facilities and institutions that had been integrated thus far. He then focused on the matter at Central High. Faubus pointed out the plan to desegregate was made before the electorate had a chance to weigh in on the situation.[27] In addition, the governor also expressed several concerns he had regarding the decision to integrate Central:

1. Virgil Blossom had appealed to him for protection.
2. A telephone campaign of "massive proportions" was underway to assemble white mothers at Central the next morning.
3. Caravans were descending on Little Rock from various parts of the state.
4. The governor's office had received phone calls expressing fear of violence.
5. Large numbers of weapons, such as guns and knives, had been sold to Negro youths.
6. Revolvers had been taken from high school students, both black and white.
7. Litigation over state segregation laws had not been concluded.[28]

There was no doubt the Mothers' League had started their phone tree for the purpose of assembling their membership on the grounds of Central High in protest. And there were, in fact, large numbers of segregationists from inside and outside Arkansas converging on Little Rock. However, there was no evidence any youths were buying "guns and knives" as the governor claimed.

In his speech, Faubus invoked emergency powers and called out the National Guard to surround the campus of Central High School. "The mission of the State Militia," Faubus claimed, "is to maintain or restore order and to protect the lives and property of citizens. They will act not as segregationists or integrationists . . ."[29] It became clear to Blossom, and others, that the National Guard was there for one purpose and one purpose only—to prevent the Negro students from entering Central. This was only more apparent after Brigadier General Sherman T. Clinger, head of the Arkansas National Guard, met with Blossom in Principal Matthews's office, now converted as the brigadier's headquarters. "No Negroes will be permitted to enter," Clinger informed Blossom. Faubus had completely disrupted the normal school routine and now Blossom and his staff had just hours to sort it out before the first students arrived. Because the janitorial and cafeteria staffs were black, they also were excluded from entering Central that morning. Blossom made several late-night telephone calls, recruiting volunteers to feed two-thousand-plus students at lunch time.[30]

Although the forces opposing the integration of Central High such as the Capital Citizens' Council and Mothers' League were few in number, their strength lay in the fact they could concentrate all of their efforts in one place, since only one school was being desegregated.[31] In addition, members of these organizations knew they had support from both within and outside Little Rock. Citizens' Councils from other southern states joined their Arkansas counterparts in the fight against integration. Little Rock's Capital Citizens' Council even started a myth that the nine children were from the north and were paid by the NAACP to integrate the school.[32] Thus, the segregationists were able to articulate their grievances effectively, whereas the portion of the white community that felt bound to obey the law and who accepted racial change did so passively.[33] Resistance to integration made the enforcement of the *Brown* decision more difficult and ultimately put Little Rock's stability to the test. It seemed as though Little Rock, thought by some to be peaceful and progressive towards race relations, was now revealing a different side of its nature.

CHAPTER 5
The First Day

The angry cry of a mob in front of Central High School was not the isolated shout of a few deceived people. It was the representative clamor of unthinking man, beginning in a whisper and swelling gradually into a stentorian roar which covered the earth.

—Reverend Robert R. Brown
Ninth Episcopal bishop of the Diocese of Little Rock (1956–1970)

CENTRAL HIGH SCHOOL Girls' Vice Principal Elizabeth Huckaby found it difficult to get to work on the morning of September 3, 1957. She was stopped at police barricades near Central and required to identify herself before being allowed to proceed into the parking lot. Jeeps and troop trucks stood where busses and cars were normally parked. She made her way through the crowd of armed guards inside the school to find the high school office a flurry of activity and thick with cigarette smoke. It now served as the headquarters for the Arkansas National Guard.[1]

Governor Faubus's Labor Day speech stated Little Rock public schools were to "operate as they had been operated in the past." In response, the Little Rock School Board issued a statement reading, "In view of this situation, we ask that no Negro students attempt to attend Central or any white high school until this dilemma is legally resolved." The school board then petitioned the federal district court asking for instruction on how to proceed.[2]

Consequently, only whites were to attend Central on the first day of classes. Acting under amended orders from the governor, the National Guardsmen were instructed to keep out *all* blacks, including Central's black janitors, maids, and kitchen staff. Like the students, they were not allowed to cross the National

Guard lines. Trying to maintain normalcy, Principal Jess Matthews issued a special bulletin to be read by teachers in their first period homeroom asking students "to mind [the National Guard] . . . treat them in a friendly manner and not interfere with them in any way."[3] As far as the faculty and staff at Central were concerned, this school year was off to a hectic start.

Meanwhile, the Mothers' League had ramped up their efforts and telephoned various members asking them to take part in a sunrise service on the grounds of Central to peacefully prevent the integration of the school.[4] Through the efforts of their diligent phone calls as well as word of mouth from the Capital Citizens' Council, a crowd of about five hundred turned out that morning.[5] Some prayed, others sang "Dixie," and one student was even seen donning a Rebel cap while waving a Confederate flag. Petitions calling for Superintendent Blossom's removal also circulated through the crowd.[6] When it was clear no black students arrived to attend classes, the crowd dispersed. This strengthened the resolve of the Mothers' League, whose members spent the remainder of the day making phone calls to recruit more people. They planned to reassemble the following day (and every day if necessary) to express their dissatisfaction with the planned integration of Central. For now, it appeared the segregationists were winning.

Upset with the failure of state authorities to adequately deal with the court-ordered integration, sixteen Little Rock clergymen publicly protested the governor's act of calling out the National Guard. In a released statement they deplored the overriding of the authority of the local school administration, the disregard of national law, and the excitation of racial tension. Blame for any violence was placed at the hands of the state government. They ended by appealing to every citizen to "unite with us in earnest prayer to God that justice will be brought about and a right example set for every child of our community. We call upon the Federal authorities to take steps that will restore public peace and tranquility."[7]

Not only were local religious leaders upset with the state's actions, but so was the NAACP, whose lawyers Wiley Branton and Thurgood Marshall appealed to Federal Court Judge Ronald Davies for assistance in this matter. Judge Davies agreed the students had a constitutional right to attend Central and directed the school board to proceed with the planned integration. Additionally, he ordered Attorney General Herbert Brownell and the FBI to investigate the state's interference with the federal court order. On the afternoon of September 3, Superintendent Blossom called leading black citizens of Little Rock and some parents of the black students to a meeting. At the request of the parents, Daisy Bates also attended. Blossom told those gathered that the black students could attend classes on September 4, but he was concerned the presence of the parents might incite violence. Therefore, he instructed the students to arrive alone the next morning.[8]

Worried about the students' safety, Mrs. Bates called Reverend Dunbar Ogden, head of the Greater Little Rock Ministerial Association, and asked him to organize a group of ministers to accompany the students the next morning. She then telephoned the Little Rock police asking for a car to meet the students and ministers at 8:30 am on the corner of 13th Street and Park Avenue. The officer said a squad car would be waiting at the intersection at 8:00, but it could not go any closer to the school as it was "off limits" to city police as long as the National Guard was stationed there. Finally, around 2:00 in the morning, Mrs. Bates called some of the parents of the black students and alerted them of the change of plans. Exhausted, she went to bed hopeful that in a few hours the students would be in the school. Unfortunately, not all of the students were contacted by Mrs. Bates ahead of time. One of them, Elizabeth Eckford, did not have a phone and consequently never got the message.[9]

Elizabeth Eckford woke up on September 4 both excited and nervous because the big day had finally arrived. In preparation for their first day of classes at Central, many of the students had gone shopping for new school clothes. However, Elizabeth and her sister made her outfit for the special occasion—a white blouse and an accompanying skirt hemmed in navy blue and white gingham. She got ready for school, grabbed her notebook, binder, and sunglasses, and walked a couple of blocks to 16th Street and Peyton Avenue. From there, she took a bus which would drop her off near Park Avenue.[10]

Elizabeth was the first of the black students to arrive at the school, just before 8:00 am. At the corner of Park Avenue, across the street from the Mobil station, Elizabeth approached three guardsmen who directed her along Park Avenue. As she walked, someone in the crowd shouted, "They're coming! The niggers are coming!" and the mob began to close in around Elizabeth. While the mob shouted obscenities behind her, scores of reporters and photographers tried desperately to capture this moment in history. A shy individual, Elizabeth did not say a word but kept walking. It was obvious the guards stationed at the school were not going to let her in. She knew if she could at least make it to the corner of 16th Street and Park Avenue, she could catch a bus and ride to safety. On her heels the relentless mob continued to shout, "No nigger bitch is getting in our school!" and "Lynch her!"[11]

Among the crowd surrounding Elizabeth were three teenage girls, who noticed the cameras and immediately followed behind her. Mary Ann Burleson, Sammie Dean Parker, and Hazel Bryan joined in the shouting and clamored for the lens of the cameras. Hazel's screaming face was captured in a photograph that made the front page of newspapers around the world, portraying her as a representation of southern resistance and racial hatred.[12] That infamous photograph was later reprinted in the *Arkansas Gazette* with an additional caption, "When hate is unleashed and bigotry finds a voice, God help us all."[13]

Elizabeth finally made her way to the bus stop at the corner of 16th Street and Park Avenue while newspaper reporters and camera men jockeyed for position, hoping to ask questions or to take her picture. Elizabeth sat silent on the bench, holding back tears. Benjamin Fine, a reporter with the *New York Times*, sat next to Elizabeth, put his arm around her, and comforted her for a brief period. This only intensified the mob's anger. Not only was Fine from the North, but he was a white man who put his arm around a black girl. The crowd shouted, "The nigger lover! We'll fix him!" and threatened to lynch him as well. Eventually, a white woman named Grace Lorch made her way through the crowd. Lorch's husband worked at Philander Smith College for blacks, and the pair were the only white members of the local NAACP. Mrs. Lorch sat with Elizabeth and then accompanied her on the bus until she reached her mother's workplace.[14]

***

As the sun rose on Tuesday morning, September 4, 1957, it promised to be another hot and humid day with temperatures near ninety degrees. Neither Thelma nor her parents had slept well the night before. For the past twenty-four hours, it seemed like the phone had been ringing constantly with periodic updates from Mrs. Bates. As Thelma awoke, thoughts of the first day of school raced through her mind. Certainly, the fact she was to be among the first black students to integrate Central High did not escape her attention. However, her thoughts quickly turned to more ordinary concerns facing a student attending a new school, such as wondering what her classes and teachers would be like and whether or not she would make any new friends on this day. She quickly ate breakfast and got dressed. Thelma was excited to wear the new outfit her mother made for the occasion—a light, sleeveless blouse with a dark, flared, crinoline "poodle" skirt. Thelma and her mother left for the school.

After a brief stop to pick up Minnijean Brown, they proceeded to the corner of 13th Street and Park Avenue, where Daisy Bates had arranged the meeting point. As the car approached the intersection, Thelma noticed the ministers and recognized some familiar faces—Ernest Green, Gloria Ray, Jefferson Thomas, and another black student named Jane Lee Hill (who ultimately did not enroll at Central and later returned to Horace Mann). Thelma told her mother good-bye, got out of the car with Minnijean, and walked over to where the other students were standing.[15] Soon after, Carlotta Walls arrived in another car and joined the others, who were chatting anxiously. The ministers, who included four white men (Reverend Ogden and his son David, Reverend Will Campbell, and Reverend George Chauncey) and two black men (Reverend Harry Bass and Reverend Z. Z. Dryver) took a moment to pray with the students. They then lined up in pairs and began the short walk up Park Avenue to the school with the white ministers in front, the students in the middle, and the black ministers bringing up the rear.[16]

As the group approached Central, the roar of a crowd became distinct. Shouts of "two, four, six, eight – we don't wanna integrate!" filled the humid morning air. When the group approached the Mobil gas station at the corner of 14th Street and Park Avenue, there was no mistaking it—a mob of hundreds was angrily shouting, "Nigger!" Young people were waving Confederate flags and older people were shaking their fists. Thelma's weak heart started racing. Even the short walk uphill on Park Avenue had been a daunting task for her, yet she remained calm. She was with friends and ministers, and she could see the National Guardsmen who she assumed were there to protect her. It seemed that if the group made it to the guardsmen, they could safely get into the school.[17]

When the group approached, the guardsmen did not move or speak. After a few tense minutes, troop commander Lieutenant Colonel Marion Johnson stepped forward and spoke with Reverend Odgen. Lieutenant Colonel Johnson told Reverend Ogden he was acting under Faubus's orders and his troops were not to allow the black students in the school. Thelma and the others remained silent. The commander repeated his order that the students needed to leave. The sound of the mob was deafening. "Nigger!" "Go back to Africa!" "We don't want you here!" rang though the air like bullets, piercing the souls of Thelma and her peers as they gazed up at the building where white students were entering with ease. The group slowly turned around and, in silence, walked to waiting cars and drove away.[18]

Thelma was devastated. She wondered what she was going to do next. She had come so far and worked so hard, only to be denied access into the school. Why was the governor doing this? Why didn't the National Guard control the mob and allow the black students in? Was she ever going to get into Central? Later that evening, she and her parents tuned into the evening news and learned how Elizabeth had been confronted by the angry mob that morning. Poor Liz, Thelma thought, as she watched the coverage of her friend bravely walking through the crowd.[19]

***

The events of that day were reported extensively in the September 5 edition of the *Arkansas Gazette*. Two pictures appeared on the front page. One was of

Thelma and the group of students in front of the National Guardsmen. The other was the infamous picture of Elizabeth walking with Hazel screaming behind her. Next to that picture was an article about Little Rock Mayor Woodrow Mann, who blasted Governor Faubus for creating turmoil in the capital city. He called Faubus's plan to bring out the National Guard to prevent violence a "hoax" and termed the governor's action as "an unwarranted interference." Mann went on to say: "The governor has called out the National Guard to put down trouble when none existed. He did so without a request from those of us who are directly responsible for preservation of peace and order. The only effect of his action is to create tensions where none existed."[20]

TIME magazine agreed with Mayor Mann and reported that Faubus was exaggerating circumstances and "almost single-handed he had created the reality of violence from its myth."[21] In an editorial featured on the front page of the September 4 edition of the *Arkansas Gazette*, the newspaper placed the blame for the disorder on Governor Faubus and urged him to faithfully carry out the court order to desegregate, warning, ". . . he should do so before his own actions become the cause of the violence he professes to fear."[22] Many of Central High's students also placed blame on the governor for starting trouble at the school. When asked how long he thought the tension would last, Ralph Brodie (president of Central's student body) replied, "It's up to Governor Faubus."[23]

By contrast, Governor Faubus did have his defenders, who attributed his actions to one who was trying to keep a lid on racial tensions about ready to explode. The governor may have predicted violence where there was none, but it was obvious a large number of Little Rock's residents were opposed to desegregation. Brooks Hays, Arkansas's Democratic US representative, concluded, "It was this sentiment rather than the threat of violence that accounted for most of the Governor's actions."[24] Some, like the Mothers' League, even blamed Superintendent Blossom for the turmoil at the school. They were angry the Little Rock School Board and administration had agreed to move forward with the integration of Central High.

Whatever the case, Orval Faubus claimed he was doing his constitutional duty as the elected head of Arkansas in calling out the troops to preserve the peace and well-being of his citizens. He was upset Judge Ronald Davies had ordered a federal investigation against his handling of the matter. Author Elizabeth Jacoway concludes that "it is more likely that Faubus initially hoped to provoke the Eisenhower administration into an action that would take him off the hook, one that would provide protection against violence while at the same allowing him to claim he had tried to hold out but had been overwhelmed by the superior might of the federal government."[25]

In a telegram to President Eisenhower late on Wednesday, September 4, Faubus stated the question at issue in Little Rock this moment was not integration vs. segregation but rather "whether or not the head of a sovereign state can exercise his constitutional powers and discretion in maintaining peace and good order within his jurisdiction, being accountable to his own conscience and to his own people." Faubus continued by stating this situation was created by Judge Davies due to his misunderstanding of the problems facing the citizens of Little Rock. He concluded his telegram by issuing a warning to the Eisenhower administration that if "these actions continue . . . then I can no longer be responsible for the results."[26]

The telegram sent by Governor Faubus and Judge Davies's federal court order of investigation had now reached the executive branch in Washington. The peaceful integration of schools that had occurred in other Arkansas locales such as Hoxie, Fayetteville, and Fort Smith would not be the case in the capital city. The media was descending on Little Rock in droves and all eyes were on Washington to see how the federal government would respond to this challenge of state sovereignty in Arkansas. What transpired over the next few weeks would pose the most serious confrontation between the states and the federal government since the Civil War. The battle lines had been drawn. Little Rock Central High School began the school year in a way no one could have ever predicted and certainly no one would ever forget.

CHAPTER 6
Showdown

Whenever normal agencies prove inadequate to the task and it becomes necessary for the Executive Branch of the Federal Government to use its powers and authority to uphold Federal Courts, the President's responsibility is inescapable.

—Dwight D. Eisenhower
Thirty-fourth president of the United States

IN ORDER FOR INTEGRATION to proceed at Central, federal assistance was going to be necessary. Besides the federal court order from Judge Ronald Davies, the White House was bombarded with letters appealing President Eisenhower to intervene. One such letter came from legendary baseball figure Jackie Robinson. In a September 13 letter to Eisenhower, Robinson urged the president to act. "It appears to me now," Robinson stated, "that under the circumstances the prestige of your office must be exerted. A mere statement that you don't like violence is not enough. In my opinion, people the world over would hail you if you made a statement that would clearly put your office behind the efforts for civil rights."[1]

Not only were events in Little Rock spiraling out of control, but other cities encountered disorder and violence as well. On September 9, six black students trying to enroll at North Little Rock High School were denied entrance by a large crowd of whites. Little Rock police officers remained on the sidelines, neither preventing the black students' entrance to the school nor offering them any protection from the crowd. On the same day, outside of Phillips High School in Birmingham Alabama, Reverend Fred Shuttlesworth was beaten while trying to enroll his daughter and other black students. In Nashville, Tennessee, black children were allowed to attend a public elementary school, but only after stones, sticks, and bottles were thrown at them. As a result, several white parents were arrested, and hundreds of others withdrew their students due to the violence.[2]

Many in Washington wondered how the events in Little Rock would affect America's image in the ongoing Cold War with the Soviet Union. Numerous US embassies, including those in Denmark, Brazil, and the Netherlands, sent telegrams to the State Department detailing the impact the crisis in Little Rock was having on an international level. One embassy, in Mozambique, criticized the United States by saying America's moral standing had been "considerably damaged." They went on to label any advice on African affairs given by the United States to European governments "hypocritical."[3] Pro-communist literature abroad relished the controversy caused by the issue of school integration. The Italian communist newsletter, *L'Unita*, sneered, "It is hard to imagine a country where the new scholastic year opens in an atmosphere other than serene, where the thought of desks, notebooks, and blackboards is mingled with visions of rifles, tear gas, spring knives and clubs . . . Such a country does, however, exist, and it bears the high-sounding name of 'United States of America.'"[4]

The growing discontent over the issue of school integration prompted Eisenhower's attorney general, Herbert Brownell, to act. On September 9, the Justice Department filed a petition for an injunction against Governor Faubus, General Sherman Clinger, and Lieutenant Colonel Marion Johnson of the Arkansas National Guard for interfering with the court's order to desegregate Central High School. The injunction called for the governor to comply with federal orders and remove the National Guard from Central High immediately. A hearing was scheduled in Little Rock for September 20. In the meantime, Faubus held firm, refusing to remove the guardsmen from the school.[5]

Representative Brooks Hays, up for re-election in 1958, did not want an embarrassing situation dogging him throughout the campaign. He called his friend and White House Chief of Staff Sherman Adams to arrange a meeting between the president and Governor Faubus. The two met on September 14 at the president's summer home in Newport, Rhode Island, and talked for about twenty minutes behind closed doors in the president's office. They then continued the discussion in the outer room with Congressman Hays, Attorney General Brownell, and others.[6]

The two-hour meeting resulted in mixed messages. Faubus believed he had convinced Eisenhower to postpone the integration, while at the same time agreed that the *Brown* decision was the law of the land. Claiming the need to protect the citizens of Little Rock, the governor told the president the troops were necessary. In a statement released immediately after the meeting, the governor stated, "It is my responsibility to protect the people from violence in any form.

As I interpret the President's public statements, the national administration has no thought of challenging this fact."[7] Eisenhower, however, mistakenly thought he had persuaded Faubus to go home and allow the black students into Central under the protection of the National Guardsmen.[8] In his diary, Eisenhower noted that if Faubus did not defy the Supreme Court ruling, he would not expose the governor to the humiliation that would result from challenging federal authority. "He seemed to be appreciative of this attitude," Eisenhower wrote, "and I got definitely the understanding that he was going back to Arkansas to act within a matter of hours to revoke his orders to the Guard to prevent re-entry of the Negro children into the school."[9]

Back in Little Rock, the scheduled injunction hearing convened at the federal district court on Friday, September 20. Present were NAACP lawyers Wiley Branton and Thurgood Marshall, Daisy Bates, and a few of the Little Rock Nine with their parents. After being overruled by Judge Ronald Davies repeatedly during the hearing, attorneys representing Governor Faubus shocked everyone by gathering up their papers and walking out of the court.[10] Judge Davies signed a four-page injunction which restrained Governor Faubus, as well as General Clinger and Lieutenant Colonel Johnson, from obstructing or preventing the constitutional right of the black students from attending Central High School. That evening, Faubus gave an order to withdraw the National Guard. President Eisenhower called the governor's decision "a necessary step in the right direction."[11]

Central High School began preparing its students for the changes that were coming. Superintendent Blossom issued a press statement asking all adults who were not employees of Central to stay away from the school on Monday. Vice Principal Huckaby went into Principal Matthews's office on Friday morning to discuss the proper wording for his daily bulletin to the students. The principal's message requested the students to meet the challenge "quietly,

Minnijean Brown, Terrence Roberts, and Thelma Mothershed leave the federal courtroom in Little Rock following a hearing regarding their right to attend Central High School in September 1957. (Copyright Arkansas Democrat Gazette)

courteously, and with honor for yourself and your school."[12] Late Sunday evening, Superintendent Blossom called Mrs. Bates to inform her that the nine black students could attend Central on Monday. She then relayed the good news to the parents.[13]

By this point, all nine students had been excluded from Central for a period of three weeks. During this time, the students felt as though they were in "limbo." Occasionally, they met at the Bates' house to discuss legal strategies with the NAACP or to answer questions from newspaper reporters. After the first week of classes passed, Mrs. Bates arranged for the students to obtain homework from their Central High teachers. Dr. Lee Lorch from Philander Smith College (whose wife Grace helped Elizabeth on her first day) recruited several professors and local teachers as tutors so the students could stay abreast of their schoolwork.[14]

***

Monday, September 23, 1957, dawned bright and clear. Thelma's parents dropped her off at the Bates' house on West 28th Street just before 8:00 am. She noticed scores of reporters and photographers already on the scene, eager to capture this historic moment in their newspapers and magazines. The Little Rock city police telephoned Mrs. Bates a few minutes after 8:00 to inform her they would provide an escort for the students. Thelma was relieved to hear this news, as Mayor Woodrow Mann had issued a statement the day before promising a contingent of police at Central High School "as long as necessary to deal with any effort by mob leaders to breach the peace of this community."[15]

While Thelma and the others were waiting at the Bates's house, she observed four black reporters having coffee and visiting with Mrs. Bates. They were L. Alex Wilson, managing editor of the *Memphis Tri-State Defender*; James Hicks of *New York Amsterdam News*; Moses Newsom of Baltimore's *Afro-American*; and Earl Davy, a photographer for the *Arkansas State Press*, which was owned and operated by L. C. and Daisy Bates. Assuring them their help was not needed, she sent all of the press on ahead to the school.[16] It was now around 8:40 am. "OK children," Mrs. Bates instructed the students, "it's time to go." Nervously, Thelma got into the car with Mr. and Mrs. Bates. Several other students joined her while the rest piled into a car driven by a member of the NAACP. The group then made the short trip to Central.

***

Approximately seventy Little Rock policemen stood idly behind sawhorse barricades at Central High School. A crowd had begun to form in front of the school as early as 6:00 am. There were curious bystanders as well as many others who were there specifically to prevent the nine students from entering the school. A later analysis of mob participants revealed more than half of the crowd that morning were young, high school-aged men from Pulsaki County, which included not only Little Rock but North Little Rock as well. It was believed many North Little Rock residents participated because they hoped to thwart the integration at Central just as they had at their own school earlier in the month.[17] The Lemon family was among the participants. Fred Lemon was at work during the morning of September 23; however, his wife and children took part in the mob. Despite the fact that none of the Lemon children ever attended Central but rather went to North Little Rock schools, they all felt a personal and emotional commitment to the cause. Mr. Lemon, interviewed by *LOOK* magazine, stated, "Segregation is our way of life, and we are fighting for it."[18]

Daisy Bates fields questions from reporters in front of her home. Surrounding her are (left to right) Elizabeth Eckford, Minnijean Brown, Melba Patillo, and Thelma Mothershed. (Photo by Thomas McAvoy/The LIFE Picture Collection/Getty Images)

The car carrying Alex Wilson and the other black reporters arrived just seconds ahead of the students. As they exited their car, the mob mistook the reporters for parents of the black students and started yelling, "Look, here they come!" About twenty whites began to chase the four reporters. Wilson, a tall ex-Marine who covered the Emmett Till lynching trial in Mississippi in 1955, decided not to run and was brutally attacked. Someone threw a brick and hit Wilson on the back of his head, causing him to fall. *LIFE* magazine displayed photos in a two-page spread of Wilson's attack by the mob, showing him being strangled and kicked.[19] Ultimately, due to this attack, he suffered from chronic headaches and later was diagnosed with Parkinson's disease. He died three years later, in October 1960, at the age of fifty-one.[20] However, the unexpected diversion of Wilson's attack permitted the cars carrying the nine students to pull up along the 16th Street side entrance almost undetected, thus allowing the students safe passage into the school.

It wasn't long before five Central High female students rushed out of the school screaming, "They got in! The niggers are in our school!" They started yelling for the other students to join them outside. Soon, about thirty to fifty other students joined the crowd, which had now grown close to a thousand people. An announcement made in the homerooms concerning the upcoming football game against Baton Rouge caused the students to cheer. Mistaking the noise for violence, twenty white men tried to rush past the police and into the school, yelling, "Let's get them!"[21]

***

To Thelma, whose five-foot-four-inch frame was dwarfed by the high ceilings and walls, Central seemed larger than life. She looked at the other members of the Nine, and like her, they all were smiling. It wasn't long before a young well-dressed male student approached the group. He greeted them cheerfully. "Hi. My name is Craig Raines. Welcome to Central." Craig, a member of the student council, escorted the Nine down to Principal Matthews's office where Vice Principal Huckaby was waiting.

Suddenly, Thelma began to feel faint. Her anxiety that day, combined with the distance she had walked, was too much. She turned blue and immediately sunk to the floor. Vice Principal Huckaby helped her down into a chair. "Quick," Huckaby instinctively told one of the office aides, "go get some water and the nurse!" Soon, Nurse Carpenter arrived, sat next to Thelma, and applied a cold cloth to her head. "Are you alright?" the nurse asked. "Uh-huh," Thelma acknowledged in her weakened state. "Do you want to go home?" Thelma's thoughts immediately turned to her parents and how she did not want to worry them. Summoning up her courage, Thelma said, "No, I'll be alright."[22]

Just at that moment, Principal Matthews came in to welcome the nine students. He led the other eight students to the outer office and gave them their schedule cards. At about 9:15 am, after the halls were clear and the tardy bell had rung for first hour, Principal Matthews escorted the students to the guidance director's office. Thelma remained behind while Nurse Carpenter checked her pulse and blood pressure. After a few minutes, Vice Principal Huckaby checked on Thelma. "How is she doing?" Huckaby asked. "Her pulse is still irregular," the nurse replied. "I'll see that she gets to her first period class when she is able."[23]

Inside the school, the next couple of hours were routine. The nine black students went to first and second periods. A few angry students walked out of their classes, but otherwise there were no reported incidents. Later, Thelma recounted the day for a reporter from the *Arkansas Democrat*. "Nothing much happened at all. I went to three classes. There was no shouting or anything. Neither the teachers nor most of the students acted like they resented having us there. We didn't pay too much attention to the commotion going on in the halls."[24]

Outside the school, a different story was unfolding. Since learning the students had successfully entered the school, the mob became restless. They turned their anger on the white journalists. Paul Welch, a reporter for *LIFE* magazine, and two photographers, Grey Villet and Francis Miller, were verbally and physically assaulted. In addition, equipment was taken from them and destroyed.[25] The police had a difficult time containing the mob, whose members were threatening to storm into the school and lynch the black students. It was becoming evident that the situation was unsafe. It was only third period, but Deputy Chief of Police Gene Smith communicated to Principal Matthews that he should send the black students home for the day. Thelma was in her French class when a school official burst in. "Thelma," she said, "you have to go now. Take your books." The class fell silent as Thelma picked up her belongings and left the room. "What is going on?" she asked. "The principal is sending you and the others home for your own safety."[26] The nine students were rushed down to the basement garage and instructed to get into a couple of sedans. Terrence Roberts, one of the students, recalls, "We were told to move very quickly. They told us to put notebooks against the windows and keep down . . . Whatever we did say to each other was spoken in hushed tones as we watched the mob milling around the school."[27] The students were driven back to Mrs. Bates's house.

Upon hearing Thelma suffered an attack that morning, Mrs. Bates informed Mrs. Mothershed of what had happened. Mrs. Bates learned a minister at the Mothersheds' church had offered Thelma a scholarship to attend an integrated school in his home state of Oklahoma. Daisy Bates suggested perhaps it would be best if Thelma considered accepting the minister's offer. "No," Hosanna Claire adamantly replied. "Thelma has made up her mind. What I will do is contact the school authorities and see if they can arrange Thelma's classes so she won't have to climb so many stairs."[28]

***

Governor Faubus was conveniently out of town attending a Southern Governors Conference in Sea Island, Georgia. In Washington, President Eisenhower received a telegram from Mayor Mann informing him of the day's events and that, due to the mob's actions, the black students had to be removed from Central. Eisenhower then issued Proclamation 10730 which ordered the mob to "cease and desist" their obstruction of justice and ordered them to disperse.[29] In the meantime, Daisy Bates announced to the press that, for the students' safety, she was not going to bring them to school the next day. Fearing mob violence, many parents kept their children home from school on Tuesday, September 24, as well.

Although a mob once again formed outside of Central on Tuesday morning, it dwindled throughout the day and the newspapers reported it orderly as compared to Monday's crowd.[30] In spite of these reports, Mayor Mann sent an anxious telegram to President Eisenhower pleading for him to send federal troops: "THE IMMEDIATE NEED FOR FEDERAL TROOPS IS URGENT. THE MOB IS MUCH LARGER IN NUMBERS AT 8AM THAN AT ANY TIME YESTERDAY. PEOPLE ARE CONVERGING ON THE SCENE FROM ALL DIRECTIONS. MOB IS ARMED AND ENGAGING IN FISTICUFFS AND OTHER ACTS OF VIOLENCE. SITUATION IS OUT OF CONTROL AND POLICE CANNOT DISPERSE THE MOB."[31]

Eisenhower was furious. No longer evading the issue, he conferred with Attorney General Brownell. "Well, if we have to do this," he told Brownell, "then let's apply the best military principles to it and see that the force we send there is strong enough that it will not be challenged . . ."[32] He signed an executive order activating over one-thousand riot-trained paratroopers of the 101st Airborne Division from Fort Campbell, Kentucky. They were to proceed to Little Rock immediately. He also called back the Arkansas National Guard, this time under federal control. That evening, President Eisenhower addressed the nation on television. In his speech, he made it clear that "mob rule cannot override the decisions of our courts" and the federal troops were being sent there not to relieve local authority or run the school, but for the purpose of "preventing interference with the orders of the court."[33]

When Governor Faubus returned to his capital city that evening, he told reporters he felt like General Douglas MacArthur. "I've been relieved of my job." Faubus also felt vindicated for originally calling out the guardsmen because once they were gone, his prediction of violence came true. Now the federal government was forced to enforce its *own* rule. Faubus believed Attorney General Brownell wanted to use troops all along and was just looking for a reason. Indeed, when later interviewed for the award-winning PBS documentary *Eyes on the Prize*, Brownell admitted, "We felt that this was the test case that had to be made in order to dramatize to everyone that when it came to a showdown the federal government was supreme in this area."[34]

Whether it was due to personal or political motives on behalf of federal, state, and/or local authorities, the damage was done. Little Rock, Arkansas, was to become an occupied territory as federal troops were called into a southern state for the first time since Reconstruction. Some saw this action as an unwarranted invasion of the state by the federal government. Others saw it as a necessary means to ensure the constitutional rights of ordinary citizens. Caught in the middle were nine black teenagers who just wanted an education.

CHAPTER 7
Going Off to War

Any time it takes 11,500 soldiers to assure nine Negro children their constitutional rights in a democratic society, I can't be happy.

—Daisy Bates
President of the NAACP, Arkansas Branch (1952–1961)

AS THE 101ST AIRBORNE made its way into Little Rock and onto the grounds of Central High School on Tuesday, September 24, Daisy Bates was busy fielding questions from reporters who descended upon her house. Everyone wanted to know if the Little Rock Nine were going to school the next day. Awaiting instructions from Superintendent Blossom, Mrs. Bates delayed calling the parents. However, it was now 10:00 pm, and still with no word from the administration, she called and said the students were to stay home.

Shortly after midnight, the call from Superintendent Blossom finally came. He stated Major General Edwin Walker, chief of the Arkansas Military District in command of the 101st and the newly federalized National Guardsmen, was requesting to have the students arrive at Central in the morning. Mrs. Bates informed him she had already told the parents the students *weren't* coming and usually they took their phones off the hook after midnight to avoid harassing calls. Superintendent Blossom instructed her to go door to door and said Edwin Hawkins (principal of Dunbar Jr. High) and Leroy Christophe (principal of Horace Mann) would assist her. It took nearly three hours, but the trio made it to each of the houses to inform the parents that indeed their children were to go to school that morning.[1]

The nine students assembled at the Bates' house around 8:30 am and waited. Finally, around 9:00, four US Army jeeps arrived and were stationed on 28th

Street, two at each end of the block. Paratroopers exited the jeeps and stood guard as an army station wagon pulled up in front of the Bates's house. "Mrs. Bates, we're ready for the children," the soldier said as he opened up the car door for the students. Mrs. Bates and the parents, with tears of joy streaming down their faces, watched as the jeeps and station wagon left the house. With guns mounted and rifles bearing, the caravan made its way through the streets of Little Rock on the way to Central High.[2]

Meanwhile, Central High School looked like an army base camp that morning. Street-corner barricades had been set up from 14th to 16th Streets. About 350 paratroopers had taken up strategic positions around the perimeter of the school. An army helicopter took off from the football field and was hovering overhead. Soldiers stood on the rooftop with walkie-talkies and jeeps patrolled the surrounding streets. Newsmen were allowed on the sidewalk, but other civilians were told to keep moving along.[3] Inside the school, Major General Walker addressed an assembly of students in the auditorium informing them they had nothing to fear from his soldiers and there would be no interference with their studies.

As the caravan carrying the Little Rock Nine stopped in front of the school, *TIME* magazine reported the scene. "Three platoons came on the double across the school ground, deployed in strategic positions. Another platoon lined up on either side of the Negroes . . . There was dead silence around Central High School."[4] At 9:22 am, with an escort of twenty-two paratroopers of the 101st and the eyes of the world upon them, Thelma and the other students walked up the steps and safely entered Central High School.[5]

Once inside, each of the Nine was assigned to a National Guardsman, who escorted them safely from one room to another. Most of the white students

The Little Rock Nine enter Central High School escorted by members of the 101st Airborne Division of the US Army on September 25, 1957. (Courtesy of Associated Press)

they encountered that morning were friendly and receptive; however, others walked out in protest. It was reported the office was filled with students who were signing out to leave school as the nine black students entered.[6] To add to the chaos, a bomb threat was received shortly after 11:00 am. Principal Matthews immediately announced a fire drill and evacuated the building. After no bomb was found, students were allowed back inside at noon. After an uneventful few hours, the students were returned to the Bates' house via military escort at 3:30 that afternoon.[7]

***

Thelma enjoyed a relatively peaceful first week at Central. Her small stature and mild-mannered nature did not make her as much of a target as some of the other black students. While on the front lawn during the "fire drill" on September 25, several white students were seen talking and joking with Thelma and reporters observed her having a pleasant conversation with one of the teachers.[8] Over the course of the next couple of days, Thelma settled into her classes. Except for biology class, where she was assigned to be Jefferson Thomas's lab partner, she did not see the other black students other than at lunch. A. L. and Hosanna Claire joined the other parents in signing a telegram to President Eisenhower, thanking him for his handling of the situation. A few days later, A. L. received this letter:

October 4, 1957
Dear Mr. Mothershed:

I deeply appreciate your September thirtieth telegram, signed also by other parents. The supreme law of our land has been clearly defined by the Supreme Court. To support and defend the Constitution of the United States is my solemn oath as your president – a pledge which imposes upon me the responsibility to see that the laws of our country are faithfully executed. I shall continue to discharge that responsibility in the interest of all Americans today, as well as to preserve our free institutions of government for the sake of Americans yet unborn.

I believe that America's heart goes out to you and your children in your present ordeal. In the course of our country's progress toward equality of opportunity, you have shown dignity and courage in circumstances which would daunt citizens of lesser faith.

With best wishes to you,

Sincerely,
Dwight D. Eisenhower[9]

Thelma Mothershed kept up with her studies during the integration year at Central High School. (Courtesy of the Wisconsin Historical Society/WHS-52744)

The majority of Thelma's teachers treated her fairly. One notable exception was her homeroom teacher. Unfortunately, Thelma had to endure this woman's anti-integration attitude at the beginning of every school day. On one occasion, Thelma arrived late to class with a pass from Mrs. Huckaby's office. This teacher demanded Thelma place the pass on the desk. Next, she dragged it over with a pencil to sign it and then moved it to the edge of the desk for Thelma to pick up. She wouldn't allow any sort of physical contact with Thelma, even the exchange of a school pass. "I don't know what she was afraid of – it wasn't like the color was going to come off," Thelma later joked.[10]

***

President Eisenhower's order to call out the army and federalize the guard drew mixed reactions from Little Rock's citizens. Many sided with Governor Faubus's opinion that Little Rock had become an occupied territory. "In the name of God whom we all revere," Faubus lamented, "what is happening in America?"[11] The Mothers' League bombarded the governor's office with demands to close the school. In South Carolina, Senator Olin Johnston stated, "If I were governor and [the president] came in, I'd give him a fight such as he has never been in. I'd proclaim a state of insurrection."[12]

On the other hand, some praised the president for his actions. "History may find it fantastic," a *LIFE* magazine editorial read, "that a grown man was willing to use state troops to keep nine children out of school. But the president of the United States is writing the new history that says, now and for all time, that such defiance will not be tolerated in a free nation that lives by law."[13] Soon after the troops arrived in Little Rock, letters of support began to pour in at the White House. The Little Rock Chamber of Commerce wrote, "We are gratified with your deep concern, your patience, and your apparent understanding of our situation and its complexities."[14] In another letter, Harold Engstrom, a member of the Little Rock School Board who supported integration, stated the president's actions had been "most appropriate and accurately analyzed" and "the student's [sic] education at Central High School would have been warped had you done otherwise."[15]

While President Eisenhower may have been confident in his actions, the presence of troops at Central did not alter the fact that the threat of violence still persisted, both inside and outside of the school. Over a period of several months, Central's administration dealt with at least forty-three bomb threats.[16] Not all of the calls were hoaxes, however. One night, Superintendent Blossom was called out to the school to assist the police in removing a homemade bomb from one of the lockers. Blossom remembered, "The fuse was lighted just after school was dismissed for the day, but the fire had gone out before it reached the bomb. On two other occasions we found similar home-made bombs that had not been lighted . . . and one morning while school was in session we found two sticks of dynamite."[17]

As the school year progressed, bullying of the Little Rock Nine intensified. A core group of about one-hundred to two-hundred white students devised numerous attacks on the Nine, including pushing them down stairs, striking them with fists, kicking them, dumping food on them, and spitting on them.[18] The worst torture, however, was meted out in the locker rooms during gym class, where the armed guards were not allowed. Elizabeth Eckford remembers in her gym class, a typical routine involved whites flushing all the toilets at once while the she was in the showers, thus scalding her terribly.[19]

Since the media focused on what was happening *outside* of the school rather than inside, most Americans assumed the guards were preventing any kind of violence aimed at the black students. Indeed, the newspapers reported the school was "quiet" as the Nine finished the first week.[20] When the news of the Russian *Sputnik* replaced the events of Little Rock on the front pages of newspapers, the assumption was made that all remained calm at Central. As a result of this misguided thinking, the president recalled several hundred members of the 101st Airborne on September 30 to Camp Robinson about twelve miles from Little Rock. This action left the federalized guardsmen in charge and, as a result, the next few days were called the "roughest" the students had faced since entering Central.[21]

On Wednesday, October 2, the Nine had to enter the south side entrance on 16th Street as the main entrance was full of segregationist students who were shouting and would not let them pass.[22] Later that same day, Jefferson

Thomas and Terrence Roberts were attacked by bullies who knocked books out of their hands and kicked them. The National Guardsmen, just six feet away from the altercation, saw the attack but did nothing to stop it or protect the two boys.[23] This inaction by the guardsmen just emboldened other white students to intimidate the Little Rock Nine.[24] For example, following a pep assembly that Friday, a group of boys pinned Melba Patillo up against a darkened wall in the auditorium's balcony. Choking her, the boys hissed, "We're gonna make your life hell, nigger. You'all are gonna go screaming out of here, taking those nigger-loving soldiers with you."[25]

As the weeks turned into months, the president was receiving more criticism from state officials regarding his use of troops. Giving in to the pressure, Eisenhower removed the 101st Airborne completely from Little Rock. The order, which came in November of 1957, also stipulated the National Guardsmen were to remain only on the *outside* of the school. Now the Little Rock Nine were on their own against the segregationists. It was at this point Jefferson Thomas was seriously hurt when he was knocked out during a particular altercation.[26]

Throughout the following weeks, attacks on the black students intensified. Elizabeth Eckford later said that by the springtime, the Nine didn't even bother to report the bullying because the administration wouldn't do anything about it and didn't believe them when they did report it.[27] The Little Rock Nine and their parents also suffered psychological trauma due to the segregationists. One such bully followed Gloria Ray around the halls swinging a rope shaped in a hangman's noose.[28] Terrence Roberts remembers his mother receiving a phone call stating he had been savagely beaten and he had a short time to live. She rushed to Central only to find her son sitting in class unharmed.[29] Ernest Green, the only senior of the group, said after the guards left, there were more bomb scares and lynching threats. He recalls one instance when white students put broken glass on the steaming shower room floors for the black students to step on. "Going to school," Green stated, was like "going off to war."[30]

***

Thelma was exempt from taking PE because of her health condition and as a result didn't endure as much torment as the other students. However, she had her share of encounters with the bullies as well. One day, as Thelma was coming down the stairs, someone spat on her. On another occasion, Thelma came home and discovered she had ink on her blouse, and it was ruined. Often, Thelma was stuck by pins that protruded from the bullies' notebooks.

One day, Thelma was called into Mrs. Huckaby's office after being accused of kicking another student. When questioned, Thelma said, "I have never kicked anybody and would not treat someone like that." Mrs. Huckaby glanced at both girls and then asked Thelma, "Well, what do you say to her?" Thelma looked at her accuser. "*IF* I kicked you," she replied in a non-confrontational manner, "I apologize." Huckaby then called the accuser's parents to explain the incident. Even though the girl was willing to accept Thelma's apology, the mother lashed out, "You mean a nigger girl kicked my daughter? I'm getting a lawyer." Mrs. Huckaby then called for the school nurse, who noted no bruising or abrasion on the girl's leg. The incident was reported by the *Arkansas Gazette* the following day; however, no charges were pursued and the matter was later dropped.[31]

In spite of these incidents, Thelma refused to tell her parents of the suffering she was forced to endure. She felt these battles were hers to fight and did not want to worry them. Her younger brother Michael remembers Thelma's attitude as always positive. "Dinnertime conversation," he said, "never centered on her day at school."[32]

***

After the 101st Airborne paratroopers had been removed, and with no armed guards for protection of the black students inside the school, segregationists resumed their task of trying to remove the Little Rock Nine. Melba Patillo Beals later stated, "Segregationists urged Central High's student leaders to antagonize and taunt us until we responded in a way that would get us suspended or expelled."[33] Their goal would be achieved when one of the nine students, Minnijean Brown, was suspended and later expelled. An outgoing and spirited individual, Minnijean was targeted by white students because they believed she walked the halls as if she "belonged" there.[34] Superintendent Blossom believed Minnijean, while intelligent, was quick tempered and looked upon her as a troublemaker. When harassed by white students, she retaliated and thus was targeted more than some of the other black students.[35]

In November, Minnijean was suspended following an incident in the cafeteria. Several boys were kicking their chairs out into the aisle, hitting her legs as she made her way through the cafeteria tables with her lunch tray. After repeated hits, Minnijean eventually dropped the tray, accidently spilling the contents on her perpetrators. The kitchen staff, all black, broke out in applause.[36]

In February, she was expelled after an argument with a girl named Frankie Gregg. Frankie hit Minnijean in the back of the head with a purse full of combination locks. "My teacher didn't see the purse when it hit me on the back of the head," Minnijean remembers. "She saw it when I picked it up, decided what to do with it, dropped it again, and said, 'Leave me alone, white trash.'"[37] Having successfully removed one of the black students from Central, segregationist students began passing out cards. One of them simply read, "One Down . . . Eight to Go."

***

As the weeks progressed, Thelma's parents began to receive more threatening phone calls. "Some boys called my house at night and told my family 'If that nigger comes back to school again, we'll blow your house up.' So, the last person to go to bed just took the phone off the hook," Thelma remembers. A. L. and Hosanna Claire did their best to shelter their other children from the threats of these white segregationists, but everyone in the Mothershed household knew the tension was mounting.

Thelma's worst day occurred in mid-February after several inches of snow had fallen. Schools around Little Rock were dismissed early, a rarity for that community. Michael Mothershed, Thelma's younger brother, was home from kindergarten watching television when Hosanna Claire came into the living room. "What's going on?" asked Michael. His mother hurriedly put on her coat. "We have to go pick up your sister from school," she replied. Michael's older brother Gilbert had just arrived home from Horace Mann, so the trio headed to Central to pick up Thelma, Minnijean, and Melba.

The girls were at the 14th Street side entrance, waiting on their ride when they noticed a group of boys nearby laughing and taunting. Hosanna Claire pulled up beside the school and Thelma, Minnijean, and Melba began walking toward the car. Suddenly, Thelma was hit in the head with a snowball. The boys had taken rocks and packed snow around them and were hurling them at the girls. One of the rocks hit the car window, causing it to crack. The National Guardsmen on duty witnessed all of this but did not intervene. Gilbert wanted to get out of the car and fight the boys, but his mother told him to "stay in the car." Thelma remained quiet on the ride home, but when she got to her bedroom, she closed the door, threw her books on the bed, and sobbed.[38]

CHAPTER 8
The Lost Year

I have determined that domestic violence within the Little Rock School District is impending, and that a general, suitable, and efficient educational system cannot be maintained in the senior high schools of the Little Rock School District because of the integration of the races.

—Orval Faubus
Thirty-sixth governor of Arkansas (1955–1967)

DESPITE THE PHYSICAL AND VERBAL ABUSE at Central High School, the eight remaining black students persevered through the final months of the 1957–1958 school year. As the graduation date approached for the sole senior of the group, Ernest Green, harassment of the other black students intensified. Melba Patillo Beals recalled Vice Principal Huckaby suggested during exam week the black students come to school only to take finals and then leave immediately. Word spread quickly that the school board was hiring extra security guards for the hallways and Little Rock police, federalized Arkansas guardsmen, and perhaps even the FBI would be on hand during the graduation ceremony in case any threats of violence manifested themselves.[1]

On Tuesday evening, May 27, 1958, between four-thousand and five-thousand people assembled at Quigley Stadium for Central's graduation ceremony. Police and detectives were not only watching the grounds of Central High, but also monitoring the homes of Superintendent Blossom and Principal Matthews. Like Ernest Green, their homes and families were also threatened if indeed a Negro student received a diploma from Central. For their own safety, the other black students were advised not to attend the ceremony. Ernest's family was present, as was a special guest—Dr. Martin Luther King Jr. Green was one of 602 graduates being honored that night. One member of the Little Rock Nine, Carlotta Walls-LaNier, and her family listened intently to the live radio broadcast. She remembered the moment when Ernest Green's name was announced and he walked across the stage to receive his diploma. "This was the most publicized commencement in history, and all of the attention boiled down to this moment. There was not a sound. No laughter, no cheers, no applause, none of the celebratory expressions that had accompanied the names of other graduates. Just silence. I exhaled as I imagined Ernie proudly walking across that stage – the first colored student ever to do so."[2]

As the summer recess began, the federal troops were officially withdrawn. Arguments over school desegregation were now limited to the courts, where the NAACP was fighting yet another legal battle against the Little Rock School Board. This time, the board had asked for a two-and-a-half-year delay of their desegregation program. In June, the federal district court complied with the board's request. Two months later, however, NAACP lawyer Wiley Branton won an appeal that resulted in an overruling of the delay. The case then proceeded to the Supreme Court, where Chief Justice Earl Warren called a special session to review the case and make a decision before the Little Rock School System began classes for the 1958–1959 year.[3]

Having recently won a third two-year term as governor, Orval Faubus received "an overwhelming endorsement of his defiant stand against the federal courts in the school integration controversy," according to the *New York Times*.[4] With this victory under his belt, Faubus called a special session of the Arkansas General Assembly on August 26 in an attempt to halt the integrationists' agenda. The legislature soon presented the governor with a package of segregation bills. Under the provisions of these bills, the governor was authorized to shut down schools that faced integration. In addition, a referendum election was to be held to determine whether voters wanted the schools to remain closed or to re-open. Faubus also had the power to withhold state funds from integrated schools and appropriate them to any accredited private or public schools in which students chose to enroll.[5]

Defying a Supreme Court ruling ordering the Little Rock School Board to proceed with the integration, Faubus quickly signed the measures, effectively shutting down all four high schools in Little Rock—Hall High, Little Rock Technical High, Horace Mann, and, of course, Central High. A referendum election was held on Saturday, September 27 to determine the fate of the four schools. The question on the ballot did not specifically indicate whether or not the schools should be re-opened but rather asked voters to choose between integration and segregation. With a 70 percent vote in favor of

Students show their disapproval of Governor Faubus's decision to close Little Rock's Central High School during the 1958–1959 school year. (Courtesy of the Library of Congress)

segregation, Faubus saw this as justification to forestall integration and keep the schools closed.[6]

Trying to deflect blame in this new crisis, Faubus showed his contempt of the Washington bureaucrats by posting a large sign outside of Central High that read, "THIS SCHOOL CLOSED BY ORDER OF THE FEDERAL GOVERNMENT." In effect, the Little Rock electorate overwhelmingly chose to shut out over 3,600 Little Rock high school students rather than let seven black students return to Central. The fate of those students, including the remaining members of the Little Rock Nine, looked bleak. This period would become known as the "Lost Year."

***

Enduring the stressful year at Central made the Little Rock Nine instant media celebrities. Several organizations wished to acknowledge them for their heroic stance in the face of racial oppression. On May 29, 1958, just two days after Ernest Green's graduation, the Little Rock Nine were flown to Chicago to participate in what would be the first of several high-profile events. Minnijean Brown joined them there, making this the first time since her expulsion that all nine had been together. On this occasion, the students received the Robert S. Abbott Award on behalf of the *Chicago Defender*, a prominent black newspaper.[7] Over five-hundred people turned out in the Cameo Ballroom of Chicago's luxurious Morrison Hotel to welcome the students. For the Nine, this was an awe-inspiring, albeit overwhelming, event. For the first time in their lives, a large crowd was there to applaud them, not to spew racial slurs or try to inflict physical harm.[8]

Next, the Nine traveled to Cleveland, Ohio. This time they received the prestigious Springarn Medal from the NAACP. Joel Elias Springarn was an educator, literary critic, and civil rights activist who served as the organization's second president. The award bearing his name is given annually to notable African Americans in the fields of politics, science, history, entertainment, and civil rights activism. Past recipients have included W. E. B. DuBois, George Washington Carver, James Weldon Johnson, A. Philip Randolph, Thurgood Marshall, and Jackie Robinson. The Nine, along with Daisy Bates, were the first-ever (and still the only) group to receive this honor.[9]

Shortly after returning to Little Rock, Mrs. Bates and the Little Rock Nine were whisked off again to New York for a special celebration in their honor hosted by the AFL-CIO Hotel Employees Union #6.[10] Over the course of three days, the students were treated like royalty. They were regaled with luxury suites at the Statler Hilton and a limousine ride to dinner at the famous Sardi's. In addition, they met with dignitaries such as Governor Averill Harriman and Mayor Robert Wagner and had lunch with United Nations Secretary General Dag Hammarskjold.[11]

One of the most exciting parts of the New York trip came courtesy of Drs. Kenneth and Mamie Clark, the couple who hosted Minnijean after her expulsion. The students were asked to dress up and told they were going to the theatre. To their surprise, the students were special guests at the new Broadway

Thelma Mothershed and other members of the Little Rock Nine meet with Mayor Robert Wagner while on a special trip to New York City in the summer of 1958. (Photo by Walter Albertin/Library of Congress)

show *Jamaica*, starring Lena Horne and Ricardo Montalban. After the show, the group went backstage where they met with the stars and received autographs. For Thelma, the highlight of the evening was getting kissed by Ricardo Montalban. She remembers she "didn't want to wash her cheek after being kissed by such a handsome man!"[12] Afterwards, the students were treated to a meal at Lindy's restaurant, a celebrity gathering spot on Broadway famous for its cheesecake. Carlotta recalled the atmosphere, noting, "Day after day we met internationally renowned entertainers and politicians, yet they treated us as if *we* were the celebrities."[13] The final day included tours of the Empire State Building and the Statue of Liberty, as well as an afternoon at Coney Island riding roller coasters. However, the extensive walking and stair-climbing involved in these tours kept Thelma from participating.[14]

As summer wound down, the Nine were again summoned, this time to Washington, DC, for the annual Elks convention. Unlike the other cities the Nine traveled to, the nation's capital was awkward to traverse, as it still practiced segregation in stores, hotels, and other public facilities. Part of this tour involved a parade in which the Nine were honored, sitting at desks with their individual names on them. Later, at a banquet hosted by the Elks, each of the Nine received a $1,000 scholarship.[15] The students also had the opportunity to tour the White House and the Supreme Court. Once again, due to the physical exertion of this type of schedule, Thelma was unable to participate. Thus, she was absent from a group photo on the steps of the Supreme Court with Thurgood Marshall, the NAACP lawyer who helped the Nine integrate Central.[16]

Back in Little Rock, A. L. and Hosanna Claire Mothershed had some decisions to make since the closing of the high schools affected two of their children. Thelma was locked out of Central and Gilbert couldn't attend Horace Mann. Like many students that year, Gilbert decided to seek his education elsewhere. He went to live with Hosanna Claire's sister, Carrie, in Greenville, Texas. With her senior year at Central now out of the question, Thelma decided to complete her education through correspondence courses offered from the University of Arkansas in Little Rock. To Thelma, the battles being waged between the State of Arkansas and the federal government were of no importance. What did matter was she was being denied an opportunity for a quality education at Little Rock Central High School . . . again.[17]

***

Feedback from the governor's proclamation that closed the four Little Rock high schools was mixed. South Carolina Governor (and former States' Rights presidential candidate) Strom Thurmond, who wrote a letter praising Faubus for his recent actions, encouraged South Carolinians to follow Arkansas's lead.[18] Little Rock high school teachers experienced confusion and disappointment. Remaining on the payroll, they were expected to report to work each day to empty classrooms. Superintendent Blossom soon instituted a "school by television" program. Beginning in late September, students were afforded thirty-minute lessons via the relatively new medium of television. Tenth graders tuned into KATV (Channel 7), eleventh graders tuned into KTMV (Channel 11), and twelfth graders tuned into KARK-TV (Channel 4) to see various Little Rock educators teaching lessons in the core subjects of English, math, history, and science.[19] While it was an innovative approach to teaching in the late 1950s, the school-by-television program was ultimately unsuccessful, lasting only one week.[20]

At the same time, individuals representing the upper-class white community of Little Rock made plans to establish a private school corporation. T.J. Raney High, a private school named for its benefactor, offered free tuition to white students only. Around eight-hundred students enrolled in the segregated school. Another less-populated private school, Baptist High, used the First and Second Baptist Churches, as well as Gaines Street Baptist Church in Little Rock, for academics and the nearby YWCA and the Little Rock Boys Club for its PE classes.[21]

Not surprisingly, parents of students who played football were worried their sons would not be able to participate while the schools were closed. Up to the 1958 season, the Central High School Tigers had an impressive, undefeated record and were ranked the best in the nation.[22] After being bombarded with phone calls from concerned parents, Governor Faubus finally agreed to their request. The previous year, Central High Head Coach Gene Hall led a football team of 130 players. Now, with only thirty-two on the roster, the Tiger football schedule continued even though the students couldn't attend Central. The Tigers' winning streak was broken in the second game of the season when they lost to a team from Baton Rouge, Louisiana.[23]

On Friday, September 12, 1958, three women assembled at the home of one of Little Rock's most influential civic organizers—Mrs. Adolphine Terry. Wife of a former congressman and considered one of Little Rock's most distinguished residents, Mrs. Terry (aged seventy-six) welcomed Vivion Brewer (aged fifty-seven) and Velma Powell (aged thirty-six and wife of Central Vice Principal J. O. Powell) into her stately antebellum mansion on that fall afternoon.[24]

The trio immediately addressed the task at hand—what to do about the students shut out of the schools. They organized what was to become one of the most influential community groups ever in Little Rock—the Women's Emergency Committee to Re-Open the Schools (WEC). The following Tuesday, September 16, the first official meeting was held in Mrs. Terry's home with fifty-eight women in attendance. To retain membership of those who preferred segregation but were influential in the community, it was decided the WEC's stated aims were not to promote either integration or segregation but to focus on re-opening the four high schools.[25]

Little Rock had witnessed rapid growth since the 1930s. However, since the integration of Central High in 1957, new businesses and families began avoiding the capital city. The name "Little Rock" became synonymous with hatred. However, as the weeks turned into months following the school closings, the WEC gained momentum. In essence, the women filled a void left by male political, economic, and civic leaders of Little Rock.[26]

Despite being harassed by the Capital Citizens' Council and denounced as traitors by their friends, the ladies of the WEC sprang into action, holding weekly rather than monthly meetings, forming committees, and engaging in massive telephone and letter-writing campaigns.[27] The ranks of the WEC were filled mostly by women in their thirties and forties who were mothers of the displaced teenagers. They were the type of middle-class women who headed church committees and served on the PTA, but who could not afford to send their children to private schools.[28] Several knew each other through these connections and were already devoted to activism within the Little Rock community. Even though many of the ladies in the WEC actually preferred a segregated society, they were not willing to sacrifice the public school system for it. They still felt a responsibility to provide an education for their children.[29]

By the end of the first semester of the 1958–1959 school year, statistics from the "Lost Year" were staggering. As reported in the *Southern School News*, 1,299 students were in private schools, 527 were getting their education through part-time correspondence courses, 1,168 were enrolled in public schools elsewhere in Arkansas, approximately one hundred were enrolled in public schools outside the state, and a staggering 604 were not getting any formal education.[30] While only 7 percent of whites chose no schooling, that number increased to 50 percent of black students.[31]

On May 5, 1959, segregationists on the bitterly divided Little Rock School Board called for firing forty-four district employees, many of whom were teachers who supported integration. After this, male civic leaders decided to join the fight. These men, some of whom had wives in the WEC, formed an organization called STOP (Stop This Outrageous Purge). Segregationists responded by forming their own organization called CROSS (Committee to

Retain our Segregated Schools), comprised of Citizens' Council and Mothers' League members among others sympathetic to their cause.[32]

Behind the scenes, STOP worked in tandem with the WEC. The men contributed their money and prestige and the WEC offered volunteers to run this new campaign. For the next twenty days, the groups went door to door and held drive-up signings of petitions to oust the segregationists on the school board and to reinstate the teachers. STOP also included a massive advertising campaign to alert and inform the public of the school board's actions and to support the teachers in question. Their efforts finally paid off. On May 25, STOP won the school board recall election. The next month the Pulaski County Board of Education appointed three new school board members and on August 12, all four public high schools re-opened. Hall High joined Central as a desegregated school.[33] Meanwhile, the CROSS campaign quickly dissolved due to poor funding, ineffectual planning, and the lack of political support among community leaders.[34]

***

In the summer of 1959, after completing her correspondence courses from the University of Arkansas in Little Rock, Thelma began applying for college admission. It wasn't long before she received news she was accepted at Southern Illinois University in Carbondale. SIUC was known for an outstanding home economics program, Thelma's desired major. However, Thelma found she was short a couple of credits and these could not be obtained through correspondence courses in Little Rock. Elizabeth Eckford found herself in a similar situation. The NAACP, concerned for Thelma and her classmates, believed the students should continue their education in a secure environment free of violence. Consequently, Thelma and Elizabeth, as well as Jefferson Thomas, were sent to St. Louis under the care of Frankie Muse Freeman, a civil rights attorney and legal counsel for the NAACP who was a close friend of Daisy Bates.[35] While the students were in St. Louis, Mrs. Freeman offered to house the girls and arranged for Jefferson to stay with a family friend. Mrs. Freeman was vigilant about keeping the media away from Thelma, Elizabeth, and Jefferson. Thus, they enrolled in the summer session at nearby Hadley Technical School to complete their coursework. Shortly after the students arrived in St. Louis, Mrs. Bates informed her friend of Thelma's heart condition, and Mrs. Freeman arranged for Thelma to be allowed access to Hadley Tech's elevator, not usually used by students. According to Mrs. Freeman, "We were always checking on Thelma to make sure she was all right, and she did fine."[36]

Upon completion of her coursework at Hadley Tech, Thelma went to Carbondale, Illinois. When she arrived at SIUC and tried to register, Thelma learned she was one credit short of the requirements needed to enter the university. After discussing the matter with her admissions officers, it was decided Thelma could indeed enroll at the university, provided she take a course in home economics at the nearby University High School. In her first semester at SIUC, Thelma found herself in the awkward position as both a high school student and a college student. When she completed her necessary coursework at University High, her transcript was sent to Central High in Little Rock.

Arriving back at her dorm after classes on a chilly day in January of 1960, Thelma checked her mail and found a large envelope addressed to her from Little Rock Central High School. She eagerly opened the envelope and proudly admired its contents. It was something she had worked hard for—it was her diploma.[37]

CHAPTER 9
The Next Steps

If you can't fly then run, if you can't run then walk, if you can't walk then crawl, but whatever you do you have to keep moving forward.

—Dr. Martin Luther King Jr.
Leader in the civil rights movement

THELMA SETTLED INTO HER NEW LIFE as a student on the campus of Southern Illinois University in Carbondale, Illinois. Founded in 1869 as the state's second teachers' college, SIUC welcomed students with scenic views amidst some of the state's oldest historic sites. The school was, and continues to be, a popular destination for students from around the country. Inspired by a former teacher, Thelma decided to pursue a degree in home economics and SIUC offered one of the best programs. The counselors at SIUC were very helpful in accommodating Thelma's medical condition by scheduling her classes so she would not have to do a lot of walking at one time. In the early 1960s, the student population at SIUC was still predominantly white, although a growing African American presence was being witnessed on campus. It was not long before Minnijean Brown, who had finished her high school education in New York, joined Thelma in Carbondale. Terrence Roberts also became a student there to pursue his doctoral degree in psychology in the late 1960s.[1]

Soon after Thelma enrolled at the university, she noticed a handsome young man who worked in the cafeteria at her dormitory. At first, it was just a wink and a smile from him as she moved through the lunch line. Later, she had the opportunity to actually meet him when her sorority, Alpha Kappa Alpha, sponsored a dance with the Alpha Phi Alpha fraternity. Across the room, she immediately recognized the man from the cafeteria. He walked over to her and introduced himself as Fred Wair. Because Thelma's heart condition prevented her from fully participating, the pair danced only the slow dances together and talked throughout the evening.[2]

***

The year 1960 saw the election of the youthful and handsome John F. Kennedy as the nation's thirty-fifth president. One of Kennedy's campaign promises included a new civil rights bill that would end segregation and ensure voting rights for blacks. Cold War concerns with the Soviet Union and his desire to appease southern congressmen who held the purse strings to his desired programs, such as space exploration, made Kennedy reluctant to move too far too fast with the civil rights issue. Since the administration's response was a slow one, movement leaders decided to take a pro-active approach at the grassroots level, hopefully forcing legislative action from the federal government.

Kennedy's first civil rights test came with the Freedom Riders—an interracial group led by the organization CORE (Congress on Racial Equality) to challenge interstate bus segregation. The group rode on busses throughout the Deep South in the spring of 1961. After riders were attacked at bus terminals by local Klansmen and with no local police enforcement, President Kennedy eventually ordered his attorney general (and brother) Robert Kennedy to provide protection via federal marshals along the journey.[3]

It was just over a year later that the young president found himself embroiled in a situation not unlike what his predecessor faced in Little Rock. This time, a Negro student named James Meredith attempted to enroll at the all-white University of Mississippi in Oxford for the fall semester of 1962 over the objections of the state's segregationist governor, Ross Barnett. Like Eisenhower before him, Kennedy had to federalize southern state troops to ensure the safe enrollment of Mcredith. Riots erupted in Oxford and Kennedy was forced to send in federal troops to restore order.[4]

More civil rights unrest followed. Dr. Martin Luther King Jr. moved his civil rights protest to Birmingham, Alabama. At the time, the city was considered to be the most segregated city in America. Dr. King's strategy involved marching in the streets to protest segregated facilities. Birmingham Police Commissioner Eugene "Bull" Connor responded by calling out police attack dogs. Mass arrests followed and soon the jails were full. Dr. King then made the bold move of allowing children to participate in the protests. This time, in addition to unleashing the attack dogs, Bull Connor ordered the fire department to disperse the marchers with water.[5]

After seeing images of children in Birmingham being rolled down the street from fire hoses, Kennedy, who had been slow to act on the issue of civil rights, decided the time had come to act more aggressively. On June 11, he appeared on national television stating, "We face a moral crisis as a country and as a people . . . I am, therefore, asking the Congress to enact legislation giving all Americans the right to be served in facilities which are open to the public – hotels, restaurants, theaters, retail stores and similar establishments." The legislation he presented before Congress eventually passed and was signed into law by President Lyndon Johnson as the Civil Rights Act of 1964. Kennedy's legacy would be defined in part by his involvement with civil rights.[6]

***

During the fall semester of 1963, Thelma was student teaching in Venice, Illinois. To avoid traveling back and forth between her school and the university, it was arranged for Thelma to stay with Mrs. Lula McShane, who lived just a block away from the school. Mrs. McShane routinely housed SIUC student teachers and had been referred to Thelma by one of her classmates. It was here on November 22 she heard the tragic news that shocked the nation—President John F. Kennedy had been assassinated while riding in a motorcade through Dallas, Texas. Like so many schools around the country, classes at Venice were cancelled and students were sent home.[7]

Thelma Mothershed around the time she was student teaching in the early 1960s. (Courtesy of Thelma Mothershed Wair)

Shortly after Kennedy's assassination, Thelma received a phone call from independent film director Charles Guggenheim. He was producing a film he hoped would counter all of the negative images from the civil rights movement. His intent was to show one story from the movement actually had a positive outcome. Entitled *Nine From Little Rock*, the eighteen-and-a-half-minute film focused on five of the Nine—Ernest Green, Jefferson Thomas, Elizabeth Eckford, Minnijean Brown, and, of course, Thelma.[8]

The setting for the story was Little Rock Central High, shown in 1964 to be integrated with blacks and whites peacefully walking and talking together in the halls. Jefferson Thomas was featured extensively throughout the film wandering the halls reminiscing of his days at Central. The film also followed Ernest Green at Michigan State University and Minnijean Brown on the campus of SIUC. Thelma's segment, too, was filmed at SIUC and showed her working on dresses in her clothing and textile class. Stand-in actor's voices provided the background commentary for Thelma and the other four characters. The film was well received and garnered an Academy Award for best short documentary of 1964.[9]

Unfortunately, when Thelma graduated from SIUC in 1964, there were few teaching jobs available and she found herself unemployed. While she did receive a few royalty checks from repeat showings of *Nine From Little Rock*, Thelma realized she needed to find work and returned home to live with her parents. Substitute teaching was all she could find, so she worked for both the Little Rock and North Little Rock School Districts. In addition to substituting, she attended Little Rock's Capital City Business College and received a certificate in bookkeeping and typing. Later, Thelma would get a job at Philander Smith College working for a few months in 1965 as an assistant secretary to the president, performing clerical work as well as serving as the switchboard operator over the lunch hour.[10]

During the summer of 1965, Thelma was introduced to Clyde Nelson. Clyde's cousin was married to a very good friend of Thelma's. Almost immediately, Clyde asked Thelma to marry him and gave her an engagement ring. She hesitated as she was not yet ready for marriage. Saving money and landing a teaching job were top priorities. The summer of 1958 had opened her eyes to new possibilities as she traveled around the country and she wanted to experience other places before settling down to raise a family. Despite all of these dreams, she accepted the ring and told friends she was engaged.

Meanwhile, Fred Wair had not forgotten Thelma. On a visit to his stepmother's family in Pine Bluff, Arkansas, he decided to look for her. A friend living in Little Rock knew Thelma's address and took him to her house. Thelma was in the kitchen doing dishes when the doorbell rang. Surprised, Thelma invited Fred in and introduced him to her mother. Soon, Fred said to Thelma, "Can I see you outside for a minute?" He took Thelma to the backyard, held her hand, and asked her to marry him. Thelma declined, as she was already engaged to Clyde.

Though rejected, Fred did not give up. A few days later, he returned to her house unannounced. He wanted to take Thelma out on a date. She indicated she had a date with her fiancé, but she would call Clyde and ask if Fred could come with them. Recalling this, Thelma smiled and said, "Clyde agreed, which was his first mistake." If he really cared about her, she wondered, why would he want Fred to hang out with them? Clyde came by and the three left together. Fred got in the front seat with Clyde and Thelma. She waited for Clyde to object. He didn't—mistake number two, she thought.

When they returned home, it was Fred, not Clyde, who opened the door for Thelma. He followed her to the door and again asked her to marry him.

She declined, but fondly remembered his kind gesture that day. Clyde seemed distant after this date and Thelma began to have doubts about their relationship. Education was very important to her and she wanted a husband who had furthered his education, which Clyde had not done. Over the next several months, Fred's persistence paid off. Thelma eventually broke off the engagement with Clyde and agreed to marry Fred. The two were wed on December 26, 1965, at Cross Street Christian Church in Little Rock. Thelma's sister Grace was the matron of honor, Lois sang, and younger sister Karen served as flower girl. Hosanna Claire made the dresses for the girls.[11]

The couple moved to East St. Louis, Illinois, in January 1966 to be near Fred's job as a science teacher at Clark Jr. High School. Since it was mid-year and no teaching positions were available, Thelma went to work at the First National Bank in St. Louis. By April, the routine of walking to and from the bus stop, balancing her job at the bank, and handling the household chores began to take a toll on her. One morning, while getting ready for work, Thelma felt dizzy and collapsed in the bathroom. Fred advised her not to go to work if she didn't feel well. She said she was okay and went on to work. While there, Thelma again became lightheaded and fainted in the restroom. Co-workers found her and immediately called Fred to come and pick her up. While waiting for him, she passed out again. Fred soon arrived and took Thelma home. The next day, Fred's brother Murphy, who lived nearby, drove Thelma to Barnes Hospital in St. Louis.

The doctors determined Thelma needed open-heart surgery, which at that time was not available at Barnes. They referred her to Dr. Denton Cooley in Houston who had the reputation of being an excellent heart surgeon. Later, Cooley would be a part of the team that assisted Dr. Christiaan Barnard in performing the first heart transplant. Nearby Scott Air Force Base provided a plane to fly Thelma to Texas. On the Monday morning after Easter in 1966, Dr. Cooley successfully performed her open-heart surgery. Once home, Thelma quit her bank job and spent

Fred Wair and Thelma Mothershed at their wedding, December 26, 1965. (Courtesy of Thelma Mothershed Wair)

the summer recuperating. That fall, Thelma finally got her first job in education—teaching home economics to eighth and ninth graders at Rock Jr. High in East St. Louis. She would hold this position for the next five years.

It was while she was teaching at Rock Jr. High that Thelma heard of Dr. King's death. Once again, assassination jolted the nation's consciousness. On April 4, 1968, the nonviolent leader of the civil rights movement was shot to death on the balcony of the Lorraine Motel in Memphis, Tennessee, while assisting striking sanitation workers in that city. Dr. King had been the guiding force of the movement from its inception. One of Thelma's heroes was gone.[12]

Meanwhile, Thelma began taking part-time graduate courses at Southern Illinois University at Edwardsville and received a masters' degree in counseling in 1972. She then left her teaching job and began her career as a counselor. For the next ten years, Thelma was assigned to provide career education counseling for students at nine elementary schools in the East St. Louis area.[13]

Once Thelma had established her new career path, she and Fred talked about having children. Doctors had told Thelma she would not be able to bear children due to her heart condition and she revealed this to Fred before they got married. After long discussions, the couple decided they would adopt a child. In early 1974, Fred and Thelma contacted an adoption service in nearby Alton, Illinois. During the interview with the adoption agency, Fred and Thelma asked to adopt a boy as soon as possible. That summer, Fred and Thelma got their wish—a boy had recently been born and was ready for adoption. Fred and Thelma welcomed their new son, Scott Frederick Wair, to their home in September.[14]

The stress from her job combined with taking care of the house and now having a young son proved to be physically demanding on Thelma. During one of her counseling visits, she noticed she had difficulty walking down the hall. Attributing the symptoms to her heart condition, doctors recommended she rest and walk with the aid of a cane. At first this seemed to help, but as time went on, Thelma started losing her balance more

Thelma Mothershed Wair celebrates after receiving her master's degree in counseling from Southern Illinois University Edwardsville, 1972. (Courtesy of Thelma Mothershed Wair)

often. One morning, as Fred was getting ready for work, he found Thelma in the bathroom, her teeth clenched and blood coming from her nose. Fred rushed her to the hospital, where doctors again believed her symptoms were heart related and treated her with blood thinners.[15]

Within a few years, the family moved to Belleville, Illinois, and Thelma returned to the classroom, teaching Foods and Nutrition from 1981 to 1986 at Lansdowne Jr. High School in East St. Louis. Later, she resumed her counseling career. During this period, Thelma continued to have issues with balance, but not as often. After a trip to Cincinnati to visit Fred's brother Jerry, Thelma complained of seeing double. She could see clearly only if she turned her head to the right and looked out of her right eye. When they got home, Thelma made an appointment to see her eye doctor, who attributed her condition to age and gave her a new prescription for her glasses.[16]

As time passed, the trouble with her balance and vision increased. After seeing new doctors who ran a battery of tests, Thelma received bad news—she was afflicted with multiple sclerosis. Doctors told Thelma she would be lucky to live ten years with this chronic condition. Multiple sclerosis (or MS) is a disease that robs the person of muscle control by attacking the central nervous system. While MS can affect people in different ways, it usually results in muscle deterioration and loss of vision.

It was clear Thelma needed to slow down. Fortunately, the Teachers' Retirement System of the State of Illinois offered an incentive for retirees so as to open up jobs for potential teachers. In 1994, Thelma took advantage of the pension package and retired from her teaching and counseling career that spanned nearly thirty years. She continued to work part-time for the next six years at the Red Cross's Second Chance Shelter in East St. Louis for homeless and abused women. No stranger to physical limitations, Thelma had always accepted challenges and moved forward. The woman who nearly forty years earlier had collapsed after climbing the stairs of Little Rock Central High on her first day of school now faced a new challenge—living with MS.

Thelma and Fred Wair and their son, Scott, circa 1980.
(Courtesy of Thelma Mothershed Wair)

CHAPTER 10
Homecoming

We all find it easy to condemn yesterday's wrong-doing, but these people stood up as children to condemn today's – and so let us learn from them and honor their example.

—Bill Clinton
Forty-second president of the United States

SHORTLY AFTER 11:00 on the morning of September 25, 1997, forty years to the day the Little Rock Nine entered Central High, Arkansas Governor Mike Huckabee stood at a podium in front of the school and introduced the president of the United States, William Jefferson Clinton. Before an assembled crowd numbering in the thousands, the president began his remarks by acknowledging the dignitaries in the audience, which included former NAACP chairperson Daisy Bates. Mrs. Bates, who had suffered a stroke a few years before, was wheelchair-bound and barely able to speak. However, she did not want to miss this historic event and listened intently as the president started his address.[1]

Over the years, the president had become very close to the members of the Little Rock Nine. Ten years earlier, in 1987, Clinton (governor at that time) invited the group to the governor's mansion, marking the first reunion of all nine members. On that occasion as well, the president delivered remarks in front of a crowd of well-wishers at Central High. This time, in 1997, was different; this time he was president. Clinton had grown up in the Jim Crow South and represented the baby boomer generation, known for its activist role during the 1960s civil rights movement. He knew this ceremony would be significant and wanted to publicly recognize the efforts of the Little

Rock Nine as veterans of the civil rights movement. He gladly accepted the invitation to speak at Central for the fortieth anniversary commemoration. Following his remarks, the president, along with Governor Huckabee, proudly and symbolically opened the front doors of Central High as the Little Rock Nine entered.[2]

Planning for the fortieth anniversary commemoration was a subject for debate among Little Rock residents. Many wondered whether the city should focus so much attention on an ugly chapter of its history they wished to forget. For the members of the Nine, it was an opportunity for the city to finally (and publicly) acknowledge its past. Carlotta Walls-LaNier, the last of the Nine to graduate from Central, contacted her eight classmates to discuss an idea with them. Careful not to portray the fortieth anniversary as a publicity stunt, she advocated that the group form a not-for-profit scholarship program. The premise of this program would be to give back to the community while at the same time promoting academic achievement. All nine agreed to donate portions of honorariums from their speaking engagements to this fund, which in turn would assist economically disadvantaged students who wished to further their education. They planned to announce their decision during the commemoration. Thus, the "Little Rock Nine" Foundation was born.[3]

***

The 1990s were a whirlwind of activities and emotions for Thelma. Beginning with the reunion in 1987, the Little Rock Nine were invited to participate in numerous ceremonies to honor them and their role in the civil rights movement. This included an invitation in June of 1990 to attend a symposium on civil rights held in conjunction with President Eisenhower's one-hundredth anniversary celebration of the former president's birth. The conference, entitled "A Decade in Black and White," was held at the Eisenhower Presidential Library in Abilene, Kansas. Carlotta, Ernest, Terrence, and Thelma represented the Little Rock Nine. Linda Brown, whose father initiated the lawsuit resulting in the historic *Brown v. Board of Education* Supreme Court case, attended as well. Interestingly, another invited guest at the conference was former Arkansas governor Orval Faubus, who greeted Thelma while she was talking to a reporter. To her surprise, he stopped and said, "Hello, Thelma!" with a big grin on his face. Shocked, she didn't know how to respond.[4]

In 1996, as the fortieth anniversary approached, Thelma received a telephone call asking if she would be willing to appear on Oprah Winfrey's show to relate her stories about the desegregation at Central. She accepted and flew to Chicago, where she was joined by some of the other members of the Little

Rock Nine. Melba Patillo Beals, who had just published her autobiography, *Warriors Don't Cry*, dominated the conversation and contributed the most. In a surprise twist, Oprah located some of the Nine's tormentors from that year and invited them to appear on the show. For the first time on national television, America witnessed an attempt at reconciliation between white tormentors and the black victims. While some questioned the sincerity of the tormentors' apologies, the episode garnered high ratings and the Little Rock Nine were back in mainstream news.[5]

As Thelma's schedule became busier, her physical limitations became more evident. It was getting harder to walk, so she relied on her cane more often. She walked without her cane at Central High for the fortieth anniversary celebration, but she held onto railings and the arm of her childhood friend Minnijean Brown-Trickey as much as possible. Fred usually accompanied her on these trips, thus helping to ease her burden.[6]

Newsweek magazine interviewed the Little Rock Nine in the lobby of the Excelsior Hotel when they returned for the fortieth anniversary celebration. The group laughed at a comment made by Minnijean. "We were thinner then!" At times, the interview was filled with emotion as the Nine recalled their memories of Central High during the desegregation. Memories evoked included Elizabeth's harrowing first day walk down Park Street and being called names and shoved into lockers.

Only the second time all of them were together in forty years, the occasion afforded them a chance to share a lot about their lives post-1958. What was most evident to this group of nine adults was that the experience at Central had a profound impact on their lives. Like many Holocaust survivors, they found themselves over the years craving anonymity and did not even tell their own children what they had endured. In many cases, their children learned about the Little Rock Nine at school rather than at home. Indeed, Thelma's son, Scott, came home from school one day and asked, "Mom, Mom, are you black history?" to which Thelma finally revealed to her son what happened to her during the desegregation year at Central High.[7]

In the months that followed, Thelma received many requests from individuals and groups asking her to speak to their organizations about her role as a veteran of the civil rights movement. One afternoon in the summer of 1998, Thelma was sitting at home when the phone rang. Picking it up, she answered, "Hello?" There was a brief silence at the opposite end. "Is this Thelma Mothershed Wair?" the voice asked. "Yes it is," Thelma replied. "Hello, Mrs. Wair. My name is Richard Hansen and I'm a history teacher at Mt. Zion High School . . ."

***

The Little Rock Nine were being summoned again—this time to the White House. An act of Congress enabled the group to be recipients of the Congressional Gold Medal. On Tuesday, November 9, 1999, the nation's highest civilian honor was bestowed on them. Just four days earlier, the group had learned Daisy Bates had passed away. While their mentor was unable to be present, family members, friends, members of both political parties and both houses of Congress, as well as representatives from the Eisenhower family were on hand to witness the event and laud their achievement.

Normally held in the House of Representatives, this time the ceremony was held in the East Room of the White House at the behest of President Clinton. *The Little Rock Nine Medals and Coins Act of Congress*, also known as H.R. 2560, noted that the Little Rock Nine:

1) voluntarily subjected themselves to the bitter stinging pains of racial bigotry.
2) are civil rights pioneers whose selfless acts considerably advanced the civil rights debate in this country.
3) risked their lives to integrate Central High School . . . and subsequently the Nation.
4) sacrificed their innocence to protect the American principle that we are all "one nation under God, indivisible."
5) have indelibly left their mark on the history of this Nation.
6) have continued to work towards equality for all Americans.[8]

Thelma Mothershed Wair and the rest of the Little Rock Nine after receiving the Congressional Gold Medal by President Bill Clinton at a special ceremony in the White House, November 9, 1999. (Copyright 1999 by United Press International)

Following remarks by Senators Dick Gephardt and Tom Daschle, Speaker of the House Dennis Hastert introduced the president. Once again, Bill Clinton enlightened the audience as to the importance of the group he had come to call friends. "When they marched up the steps of school," the president stated, "they became foot soldiers for freedom, carrying America to higher ground." The president went on to say that children are not born inherently racist. They are born to accept one another and have to be taught differently for racism to take hold. "Because so many were taught differently, it fell to these nine Americans when they were young to become our teachers. And because they taught us well," he added, "we are a better country and we honor them today. But let us not forget to heed their lessons." President Clinton then personally gave each of them the Congressional Gold Medal to sounds of thunderous applause. The Reverend Wintley Phipps capped off the event with a moving rendition of "We Shall Overcome" which, by the end, had everyone in the crowd holding hands and singing along.[9]

***

It was in the late 1990s that Thelma noticed a change in her husband, now in his fifties. She learned that at his work—he was a social worker for East St. Louis District 189—Fred had become increasingly frustrated because he was searching the building for students that had already graduated and could not find them. At home, Fred was acting even stranger. He would walk to the post office, and discovering there was no letter in the box, would return home in a rage. He was convinced someone was stealing his mail. On one occasion when he arrived home late from work, Thelma asked, "How did you get home?" "One of my students brought me," Fred replied. Thelma peered out of the window to the car in the driveway. It belonged to a co-worker of hers from the homeless shelter.[10]

Next came Fred's erratic driving. On a trip to see his brother, Fred didn't know where to turn. He also turned the wrong way when returning from Scott's house in Aurora, Illinois. When Thelma tried to correct him, Fred became agitated, wouldn't listen to her, and drove for miles in the wrong direction until stopping when he realized he was lost. Thelma had to give him directions to get back home. On another occasion, Thelma arrived late to her speaking engagement at Mt. Zion High School. Fred had gotten lost on the way, even though he had been to the school twice before.[11]

When Thelma finally convinced Fred to seek medical help, her worst fears were confirmed. In 2001, Fred was diagnosed with Alzheimer's disease. Knowing her own limitations, Thelma immediately suggested they look for a facility that could take care of both of them. Fred resisted the idea, but after several arguments, Thelma convinced him it was the right decision. In June, the couple moved into an assisted living facility in Belleville, Illinois.[12]

This created even more problems. Thelma was still working during the day and could not keep an eye on him. Fred began wandering around the building confused, yelling and frightening the other residents. Fred was shouting, "What are you doing? This is not my home!" One of the residents called Thelma to warn her that if she did not do something about Fred, the police would be called. Soon, the resident made good on her promise, causing Thelma to hurry home from work. Angry and confused, Fred was taken by the police to the hospital.[13]

Thelma resigned her job at the shelter to monitor Fred's condition, but this task was proving more difficult with each passing day. Thelma's sister Grace found a nursing home in Little Rock, so Thelma's family and friends moved her husband there. Soon, due to Fred's increasingly belligerent behavior (including biting one of the nurses), the nursing home would not let him stay. Reluctantly, Thelma had Fred moved back to Illinois to a nursing home in Cahokia that specialized in treating Alzheimer's patients.[14]

As her multiple sclerosis worsened, Thelma became unable to live independently any longer. For a year and a half, she lived with her son, Scott, and his family in Plainfield, Illinois. She moved back to Little Rock in 2002, first living with her younger sister Karen and later moving in with Grace, a registered nurse. A few times over the next three years, Grace drove Thelma to Cahokia to visit Fred, but by this time he no longer recognized Thelma or other members of the family. As she often did in times of adversity, Thelma simply accepted the situation. On May 25, 2005, Fred Wair passed away.[15]

***

The Little Rock Nine gathered yet again on August 30, 2005, as the largest bronze statue in Arkansas was unveiled. Entitled *Testament* by its creators, John and Kathy Deering, the nine life-size statues situated on the north end of the Arkansas State Capitol were the first to honor civil rights on the grounds of a southern state capitol. The statues stand within view of the governor's office as a stark reminder of how state leaders once denied their citizens basic human rights. Each of the nine has quotes emblazoned on bronze plaques circling the monument on the grounds. Thelma's plaque simply reads, "To God Be the Glory."[16]

More recognition followed this ceremony. The US Postal Service unveiled a "Little Rock Nine" stamp. Arkansas US Representative Vic Snyder, along with US Senators Blanche Lincoln and Mark Pryor, co-sponsored a bill which called for the Secretary of the Treasury to mint a commemorative coin in 2007

Testament—nine, life-size statues by sculptors John Deering and Kathy Deering that adorn the north side of the Arkansas State Capitol grounds commemorating the Little Rock Nine.

honoring the Little Rock Nine. President George W. Bush signed it into law, thus establishing the first such coin by the US Mint to honor desegregation.[17]

In 2007, Little Rock again planned celebrations, this time for the fiftieth anniversary of the desegregation of Central High. The city rolled out the red carpet for the Little Rock Nine. There was a ribbon-cutting event for a new Central High Museum and Visitor Center established by the National Park Service. The first visitor center was dedicated in 1997 for the fortieth anniversary and housed artifacts in the restored Mobil gas station near Central High School. The new visitor center, across from the old Mobil station, is an expanded version housed in a 10,000-square-foot facility on the north side of 14th Street (now known as Daisy Gatson Bates Drive). All members of the Little Rock Nine were on hand to cut the ribbon dedicating the museum on September 24, 2007.[18]

That evening, a special gala sponsored by the Little Rock Nine Foundation was held at the Statehouse Convention Center in downtown Little Rock. The event was moderated by Gwen Ifill, managing editor of the PBS program

Washington Week. In addition to the Nine and their families and friends, an array of political and civil rights icons were present, including Jesse Jackson, General Wesley Clark, Susan Eisenhower (President Eisenhower's granddaughter), and former president Bill Clinton. More than 1,300 attended the event, which raised enough money to be awarded to nine foundation scholarship winners. Each recipient was awarded $10,000 over the course of two years to help offset education expenses.[19]

Perhaps the most poignant moment of the celebration came on Wednesday morning, September 25, 2007. Just as it happened fifty years earlier, thousands of people gathered in front of Central High School. This time, however, it was a welcoming crowd that cheered and applauded as each of the Little Rock Nine was escorted to the dais by current members of the 101st Airborne Division, the same group that successfully escorted the students into the school in 1957. Each of the Nine spoke about their experiences during that year, which was the first time the entire group had ever done so at a public event. Amid multiple standing ovations, each called for continued efforts towards reaching racial equality.[20]

As he did a decade earlier, former president Bill Clinton gave the keynote address. President George W. Bush, unable to attend, issued a statement saying, "This anniversary reminds us of our Nation's struggle to fulfill its founding promise for all Americans." Referring to the Little Rock Nine, the president said, "We honor their courage, and we resolve to continue their work to make America a more perfect union."[21] After the speeches, the group was escorted to the top of the steps of Central High where they turned and waved to the cheering throngs in front of the school. Fifty years earlier they were young teenagers who risked their lives to enter the school in order to receive an education. Now, as veterans of one of the greatest social revolutions in history, the Little Rock Nine held their heads high as champions of civil rights.

President Bill Clinton congratulates Thelma Mothershed Wair with a kiss as First Lady Hillary Clinton (right) and other members of the Little Rock Nine applaud following Thelma's speech at the fiftieth anniversary commemoration at Central High School, September 25, 2007. (Courtesy Thelma Mothershed Wair)

Epilogue

What she may have lacked by way of physical strength, she more than made up for by her strength of will . . . Small in stature, Thelma towered over most all of her white student peers by virtue of her belief in the higher principles governing human interaction.

—Dr. Terrence Roberts
Member of the Little Rock Nine

WHILE IT IS TRUE THELMA and the other members of the Little Rock Nine helped advance the cause of integration, the sad fact is there are still problems concerning race and class that have transcended the boundaries of time. Today, Central High and the Little Rock School District may have a predominantly black administration, staff, and student body, but as Elizabeth Eckford told me, we should not view those statistics as an overall success on behalf of the Nine. "Central today is desegregated, but not integrated," she added. "It may be predominantly black, but courses are still segregated. Most of the students enrolled in the honors and A.P. courses are white."

While the above viewpoint may be seen as more pessimistic of the legacy regarding Central High's desegregation, perhaps a better reflection can be found in Melba Patillo Beals's autobiography, *Warriors Don't Cry*. Looking back, she stated, "If my Central High School experience taught me one lesson, it is that we are not separate. The effort to separate ourselves whether by race, creed, color, religion, or status is as costly to the separator as to those who would be separated."

In an interview with Minnijean Brown-Trickey, I gained greater insight into the event. "People made choices," she told me. "Some people chose to treat us the way they did and some people chose to sit by and do nothing to help." She warned us as historians not to focus on the specific actions against other individuals. "If we do," she stated, "we fail to learn the larger lesson of the event."

That "lesson" finally hit home for me when I traveled to Little Rock for a visit with Thelma in May of 2009. On that occasion, I took Thelma in her wheelchair to Central High, where we had a picture taken of us together. We then went down to the reflection pool in front of the school. Surrounding the pool are nine stone benches, each bearing the name of one of the Little Rock Nine. We stopped at her bench and as she reflected on her experience at Central High, I was drawn to her kindness and selfless attitude. The ability to forgive is one of the most important lessons she has taught us. Whether it was the big steps

Thelma took in 1957 to break down color barriers or the small steps she made later in life while dealing with multiple sclerosis, her spirit has never wavered.

To truly understand Thelma Mothershed's impact on the civil rights movement, one should visit the Little Rock Central High Museum and Visitor Center on Daisy Gatson Bates Drive. There, you can walk the grounds of Central High, the only active school in this country to be designated as a unit of the National Park System and once described as the "most beautiful high school in America." Inside the museum, a wealth of audio and visual information is at your fingertips. If you look closely, you will find a quote by Thelma on one of the panels: *I think race relations are better today. I hope I had something to do with that.*

Yes, you did.

The author with Thelma Mothershed Wair in front of Central High School, May 2009.

Endnotes

Introduction
1. Fon Louise Gordon, *Caste and Class – The Black Experience in Arkansas, 1880-1920*, 1.
2. Ibid., 4.
3. Eric Foner, *Reconstruction – America's Unfinished Revolution*, 368.
4. Ibid., 5.
5. Arkansas Black Code Sec.5, 1867.
6. Ibid., 57.
7. For more information on *Plessy v. Ferguson*, see Chapter 2.
8. NAACP, *Thirty Years of Lynching in the United States, 1889-1918*, 32, 41.
9. John Strausbaugh, *Black Like You – Blackface, Whiteface, Insult and Imitation in American Popular Culture*, 135.
10. Robert W. Shufeldt, *The Negro – A Menace to American Civilization*, 13.
11. Gordon, *Caste and Class*, 135.
12. Cameron McWhirter, *Red Summer – The Summer of 1919 and the Awakening of Black America*, 212-220.
13. Kenneth T. Jackson, *The Ku Klux Klan in the City, 1915-1930*, 83.
14. Ibid.
15. John A. Kirk, *Redefining the Color Line – Black Activism in Little Rock, Arkansas, 1940-1970*, 21-22.
16. Lois Mothershed-Pot, personal interview conducted May 2012.
17. Thelma Mothershed Wair, personal interview conducted December 2011.
18. Ibid., Interviews conducted October 2006 and May 2007.
19. Michael Mothershed, personal interview conducted December 2011.
20. Lois Mothershed-Pot, personal interview conducted May 2012.

Chapter 1
1. Gilbert Mothershed, personal interview conducted December 2011.
2. Lois Mothershed-Pot, personal interview conducted October 2012.
3. Thelma Mothershed Wair, personal interview conducted October 2006.
4. Gilbert Mothershed, personal interview conducted December 2011.
5. Michael Mothershed, personal interview conducted December 2011.
6. Lois Mothershed-Pot and Grace Mothershed Davis, personal interviews conducted May 2012 and August 2014.
7. Kirk, *Redefining the Color Line*, 52.
8. C. Vann Woodward, *The Strange Career of Jim Crow*, 117-118.
9. Mary L. Dudziak, *Cold War Civil Rights – Race and the Image of American Democracy*, 82.
10. David Pietrusza, *1948 – Harry Truman's Improbable Victory and the Year That Transformed America*, 78.
11. Ibid., 137.
12. Kirk, *Redefining the Color Line*, 54.
13. Ibid., 63.
14. James C. Cobb, *The South and America Since World War II*, 10.
15. Ibid., 16.
16. Thelma Mothershed Wair, personal interview conducted October 2006.
17. Ibid.
18. Michael Mothershed, personal interview conducted December 2011.
19. Thelma Mothershed Wair, personal interview conducted October 2006.
20. Ibid.
21. Kirk, *Redefining the Color Line*, 13.
22. Thelma Mothershed Wair, personal interview conducted December 2011.
23. Ibid., Interview conducted October 2006.

Chapter 2
1. *Brown et al. v. Board of Education of Topeka et al.*, 349 U.S. 294 (1955).
2. Keith Weldon Medley, *We As Freemen – Plessy v. Ferguson*, 140-142.
3. *Plessy v. Ferguson*, 163 U.S. 537 (1896).
4. *Sweatt v. Painter*, 339 U.S. 629 (1950).
5. *McLaurin v. Oklahoma State Regents for Higher Education et al.*, 339 U.S. 637 (1950).
6. Juan Williams, *Eyes on the Prize – America's Civil Rights Years, 1954-1965*, 21.
7. Waldo E. Martin Jr., *Brown v. Board of Education – A Brief History with Documents*, 25-26.
8. Jerrold Packard, *American Nightmare – The History of Jim Crow*, 235.
9. Martin, as reprinted in the "Editorial Excerpts from the Nation's Press on Segregation Ruling," *New York Times*, May 18, 1954.
10. Ibid.
11. Ibid.
12. Packard, *American Nightmare*, 239.
13. Marquis Childs, *Eisenhower: Captive Hero*, 245.
14. Cobb, *The South and America Since World War II*, 35.
15. Wyn Craig Wade, *The Fiery Cross – The Ku Klux Klan in America*, 299.
16. Packard, *American Nightmare*, 242.
17. *Brown et al. v. Board of Education of Topeka et al.*, 349 US 294 (1955).
18. Packard, *American Nightmare*, 239.
19. "A 'Morally Right' Decision," *LIFE*, July 25, 1955: 29.
20. Ibid.
21. Ibid.
22. Ibid., 30.
23. 102 Cong. Rec. 4515-16 (1956). Signed by nineteen senators and eighty-two representatives. See http://www.milestonedocuments.com/documents/view/southern-manifesto/ Accessed on July 2, 2012.
24. Ibid.
25. Woodward, *The Strange Career of Jim Crow*, 161.
26. Ibid., 166.
27. Ibid., 167.

Chapter 3
1. David Margolick, *Elizabeth and Hazel – Two Women of Little Rock*, 20-21.
2. Sara Murphy, *Breaking the Silence – Little Rock's Women's Emergency Committee to Open Our Schools, 1958-1963*, 33.
3. Elizabeth Jacoway, *Turn Away Thy Son – Little Rock, the Crisis that Shocked a Nation*, 84-85.
4. Virgil T. Blossom, *It HAS Happened Here*, 13.
5. Ibid., 15.
6. Ibid., 15-16.
7. Ibid., 16.
8. John Kirk, "Arkansas the *Brown* Decision, and the 1957 Crisis" in Elizabeth Jacoway & C. Fred Williams (ed.), *Understanding the Little Rock Crisis – An Exercise in Remembrance and Reconciliation*, 74.
9. Elizabeth Huckaby, *Crisis at Central High – Little Rock, 1957-58*, 3.
10. Ibid.
11. Ibid., 4.
12. Ibid.
13. Blossom, *It HAS Happened Here*, 198.
14. Robert R. Brown, *Bigger Than Little Rock*, 55.
15. Blossom, *It HAS Happened Here*, 27-28.
16. Daisy Bates, *The Long Shadow of Little Rock – A Memoir*, 52.
17. Ibid.
18. Huckaby, *Crisis at Central High*, 6.
19. Thelma Mothershed Wair, personal interview conducted December 2011.
20. Ibid.
21. Ibid.
22. Ibid.
23. Amy Polakow, *Daisy Bates – Civil Rights Crusader*, 41.

Chapter 4
1. I. Wilmer Counts, *A Life is More Than a Moment – The Desegregation of Little Rock's Central High*, 5.
2. Roy Reed, *Faubus – The Life and Times of an American Prodigal*, 135.
3. Ibid., 151.
4. J. Williams, *Eyes on the Prize*, 93.
5. Jacoway, *Turn Away Thy Son*, 107.
6. Blossom, *It HAS Happened Here*, 30.
7. Kirk, *Redefining the Color Line*, 103.
8. Ibid., 104.
9. Bates, *The Long Shadow of Little Rock*, 53.
10. Blossom, *It HAS Happened Here*, 45.
11. Reed, *Faubus*, 200.
12. Fletcher Knebel, "The Real Little Rock Story," *LOOK*, Vol.21, No.23, 12 November 1957: 32.
13. "Governor Georgia at Segregationist Dinner, August 22, 1957," *Southern School News*, September 1957, 7 as reprinted in *Little Rock USA – Materials for Analysis*, 32-33.
14. Bates, *The Long Shadow of Little Rock*, 4.
15. Blossom, *It HAS Happened Here*, 56.
16. Murphy, *Breaking the Silence*, 38.
17. Phoebe C. Godfrey, "Sweet Little Girls? Miscegenation, Desegregation and the Defense of Whiteness at Little Rock's Central High, 1957-1959," 152.
18. Ibid., 151-152.
19. Ibid., 158-159.

20. Bates, *The Long Shadow of Little Rock*, 56.
21. Ibid., 57.
22. "Legal Moves to Block Integration – August 29-30, 1957," *Southern School News*, September 1957, 6 as reprinted in *LRUSA*, 34-35.
23. Bates, *The Long Shadow of Little Rock*, 57.
24. Huckaby, *Crisis at Central High*, 13.
25. Blossom, *It HAS Happened Here*, 65-66.
26. Jacoway, *Turn Away Thy Son*, 122.
27. Reed, *Faubus*, 207.
28. Jacoway, *Turn Away Thy Son*, 122.
29. "The Governor's Explanation," September 2, 1957," *Southern School News*, October 1957, 1 as reprinted in *LRUSA*, 37.
30. Blossom, *It HAS Happened Here*, 75-76.
31. Kirk, "Arkansas the *Brown* Decision, and the 1957 Crisis" in Jacoway and Williams, 80.
32. Kirk, *Redefining the Color Line*, 125.
33. Kirk, "Arkansas the *Brown* Decision, and the 1957 Crisis" in Jacoway and Williams, 81.

Chapter 5

1. Huckaby, *Crisis at Central High*, 15.
2. Little Rock Board of Education, Petition to U.S. Dist. Ct. E. Ark. September 3, 1957. Reprinted from *Race Relations Law Reporter*, October 1957, in *LRUSA*, 38.
3. Huckaby, *Crisis at Central High*, 16.
4. Godfrey, "Sweet Little Girls?" 164.
5. Blossom, *It HAS Happened Here*, 77.
6. Jacoway, *Turn Away Thy Son*, 125.
7. Brown, *Bigger Than Little Rock*, 40-41.
8. Bates, *The Long Shadow of Little Rock*, 63.
9. Ibid., 65.
10. Margolick, *Elizabeth and Hazel*, 15.
11. Bates, *The Long Shadow of Little Rock*, 75.
12. Margolick, *Elizabeth and Hazel*, 45.
13. *Arkansas Gazette*, September 8, 1957: 1A.
14. Kirk, *Redefining the Color Line*, 117. See also Bates, *The Long Shadow of Little Rock*, 75, and Margolick, *Elizabeth and Hazel*, 50-51.
15. Thelma Mothershed Wair, personal interview conducted October 2006.
16. Carlotta Walls-LaNier, *A Mighty Long Way – My Journey to Justice at Little Rock Central High School*, 69.
17. Thelma Mothershed Wair, personal interview conducted October 2006.
18. Walls-LaNier, *A Mighty Long Way*, 71.
19. Thelma Mothershed Wair, personal interview conducted July 2013.
20. "Mann Attacks Story of Fear of Violence," *Arkansas Gazette*, September 5, 1957: 1A.
21. "The Meaning of Little Rock," *TIME*, Vol.70, No.15, October 7, 1957: 22.

22. "The Crisis Mr. Faubus Made," *Arkansas Gazette*, September 4, 1957: 1A.
23. Interview with Student Leader in Central High School, September 1957. Reprinted from the *Arkansas Gazette*, September 10, 1957, 4A in *LRUSA*, 43.
24. Brooks Hays, *A Southern Moderate Speaks*, 154.
25. Jacoway, *Turn Away Thy Son*, 127.
26. Telegram sent by Governor Faubus to President Eisenhower, September 4, 1957. Reprinted from the *Southern School News*, October 1957, 1-2, in *LRUSA*, 39.

Chapter 6

1. Letter from Jackie Robinson to President Eisenhower, September 13, 1957, Dwight D. Eisenhower Presidential Library Special Collections.
2. "North Little Rock Whites Bar School to 6 Negroes," *New York Times*, September 10, 1957, A1. See also "The Battle of Nashville," *TIME*, Vol.70, No.13, September 23, 1957: 14-15.
3. Dudziak, *Cold War Civil Rights*, 125.
4. "What Orval Hath Wrought," *TIME*, Vol.70, No.13, September 23, 1957: 13.
5. J. Williams, *Eyes on the Prize*, 103.
6. "Retreat from Newport," *TIME*, Vol.70, No.13, September 23, 1957: 11.
7. Statement by Governor Faubus, September 14, 1957, Dwight D. Eisenhower Presidential Library Special Collections.
8. Reed, *Faubus*, 219.
9. Eisenhower Diary, October 8, 1957, Dwight D. Eisenhower Presidential Library Special Collections.
10. Bates, *The Long Shadow of Little Rock*, 83.
11. *Arkansas Democrat*, September 21, 1957: A1.
12. Huckaby, *Crisis at Central High*, 30-31.
13. Bates, *The Long Shadow of Little Rock*, 87.
14. Thelma Mothershed Wair, personal interview conducted December 2011.
15. "Riot in Little Rock," *Detroit News*, September 23, 1957: 2.
16. Bates, *The Long Shadow of Little Rock*, 89.
17. Graeme Cope, "A Note on Crowds during the Little Rock Crisis," *Arkansas Historical Quarterly*, Vol.67, No.3, Autumn 2008, 255-257.
18. Knebel, "The Real Little Rock Story," 32.
19. "An Historic Week of Civil Strife," *LIFE*, Vol.43, No.15, October 7, 1957: 38-39.
20. Counts, *A Life is More Than a Moment*, 47.
21. "Riot in Little Rock," 1.
22. Thelma Mothershed Wair, personal interview conducted October 2006.
23. Huckaby, *Crisis at Central High*, 36.
24. "Nothing Much Happened," *Arkansas Democrat*, September 23, 1957: A1.
25. J. Williams, *Eyes on the Prize*, 106.

26. Thelma Mothershed Wair, personal interview conducted October 2006.
27. Terrence Roberts, *Lessons from Little Rock*, 105.
28. Bates, *The Long Shadow of Little Rock*, 135.
29. Presidential Proclamation 10730, September 23, 1957, Dwight D. Eisenhower Presidential Library Special Collections.
30. "Central High Quiet As Negroes Fail to Show," *Arkansas Democrat*, September 24, 1957, A1.
31. Telegram from Woodrow Mann to Dwight Eisenhower, September 24, 1957, Dwight D. Eisenhower Presidential Library Special Collections.
32. Taylor Branch, *Parting the Waters – America in the King Years 1954-1963*, 224.
33. President Eisenhower's speech to the nation, broadcast on television and radio networks, September 24, 1957, as reprinted in *LRUSA*, 65.
34. *Eyes on the Prize*, PBS/Henry Hampton/Blackside Productions, 1987.

Chapter 7

1. Bates, *The Long Shadow of Little Rock*, 101-103.
2. Ibid., 104.
3. Blossom, *It HAS Happened Here*, 120-121.
4. "The Meaning of Little Rock," 24.
5. Bates, *The Long Shadow of Little Rock*, 105.
6. "Two Men Hurt Today in Clash With the Troops at Little Rock," *Leominster Daily Enterprise*, September 25, 1957: A1.
7. See "CHS Emptied by Bomb Scare Shortly After U.S. Troops Force Integration," *Arkansas Democrat*, September 25, 1957: A1.
8. "Whites Treat Negro Pupils Friendly," *Arkansas Democrat*, September 25, 1957: A1.
9. Letter from President Eisenhower to A. L. Mothershed, September 30, 1957, Dwight D. Eisenhower Presidential Library Special Collections.
10. Thelma Mothershed Wair, personal interview conducted October 2006.
11. "The Meaning of Little Rock," 25.
12. Blossom, *It HAS Happened Here*, 129.
13. "An Historic Week of Civil Strife," 48.
14. Letter from the Little Rock Chamber of Commerce to President Eisenhower, October 4, 1957, Dwight D. Eisenhower Presidential Library Special Collections.
15. Letter from Harold Engstrom to President Eisenhower, September 25, 1957, Dwight D. Eisenhower Presidential Library Special Collections.
16. Blossom, *It HAS Happened Here*, 151.
17. Ibid., 154.
18. Reed, *Faubus*, 232.
19. Elizabeth Eckford, personal interview conducted July 2003.
20. "School Quiet, Attendance Rises As Week Closes at Little Rock," *Atlantic City Press*, September 28, 1957: A1.

21. "9 Negroes Enter Second Week at Central High School Under Guard," *Arkansas State Press*, October 4, 1957: 1.
22. "Two Negro Students Reported Beaten at CHS; Others Jeered," *Arkansas Democrat*, October 2, 1957: A1.
23. Bates, *The Long Shadow of Little Rock*, 125.
24. Kirk, *Redefining the Color Line*, 120.
25. Melba Patillo Beals, *Warriors Don't Cry – A Searing Memoir of the Battle to Integrate Little Rock's Central High*, 153-154.
26. Kirk, *Redefining the Color Line*, 121.
27. Elizabeth Eckford, personal interview conducted July 2003.
28. Ben F. Johnson III, *Arkansas in Modern America – 1930-1999*, 140.
29. Roberts, *Lessons from Little Rock*, 114.
30. Ernest Green, personal interview conducted January 2002.
31. Huckaby, *Crisis at Central High*, 156-157, and Thelma Mothershed Wair, personal interview conducted December 2011.
32. Thelma Mothershed Wair and Michael Mothershed, personal interviews conducted December 2011.
33. Melba Patillo Beals, *White is a State of Mind – A Memoir*, 11.
34. Beth Roy, *Bitters in the Honey – Tales of Hope and Disappointment Across Divides of Race and Time*, 179.
35. Blossom, *It HAS Happened Here*, 158.
36. Minnijean Brown-Trickey, personal interview conducted July 2003.
37. Elizabeth Jacoway, "Not Anger but Sorrow: Minnijean Brown Trickey Remembers the Little Rock Crisis," *Arkansas Historical Quarterly*, Vol.64, No.1 Spring 2005: 21-22.
38. Thelma Mothershed Wair and Michael Mothershed, personal interviews conducted December 2011.

Chapter 8

1. Beals, *Warriors Don't Cry*, 298.
2. Walls-LaNier, *A Mighty Long Way*, 128.
3. Kirk, *Redefining the Color Line*, 132.
4. *New York Times*, July 30, 1958, 1, excerpt in *LRUSA*, 105.
5. *Southern School News*, September 1958, 4, excerpt in *LRUSA*, 114.
6. Blossom, *It HAS Happened Here*, 185.
7. Beals, *Warriors Don't Cry*, 306.
8. Walls-LaNier, *A Mighty Long Way*, 130.
9. Ibid.
10. Ibid., 133.
11. Beals, *Warriors Don't Cry*, 306, and Walls-LaNier, *A Mighty Long Way*, 134.
12. Thelma Mothershed Wair, personal interview conducted July 2013.
13. Walls-LaNier, *A Mighty Long Way*, 135.
14. Thelma Mothershed Wair, personal interview conducted July 2013.
15. Walls-LaNier, *A Mighty Long Way*, 139.
16. Thelma Mothershed Wair, personal interview conducted July 2013.
17. Ibid.
18. Reed, *Faubus*, 246.
19. *The Lost Year – The Untold Story of the Year Following the Crisis at Central High*, Sandra Hubbard prod., Morning Star Studio, 2007.
20. Sondra Gordy, *Finding the Lost Year – What Happened When Little Rock Closed Its Public Schools*, 39-40.
21. *The Lost Year* and Gordy, *Finding the Lost Year*, 66-67.
22. *The Lost Year*.
23. Counts, *A Life is More Than a Moment*, 60.
24. Vivion Lenon Brewer, *The Embattled Ladies of Little Rock, 1958-1963 – The Struggle to Save Public Education at Central High*, 8.
25. Ibid., 10, 13.
26. Murphy, *Breaking the Silence*, 58-60.
27. Brewer, *The Embattled Ladies of Little Rock*, 45.
28. Murphy, *Breaking the Silence*, 74.
29. Karen Anderson, *Little Rock – Race and Resistance at Central High School*, 152-153.
30. *Southern School News*, January 1959, 14, excerpt in *LRUSA*, 132.
31. *The Lost Year*.
32. Anderson, *Little Rock – Race and Resistance*, 186-187.
33. Gordy, *Finding the Lost Year*, 143, 153-154.
34. Anderson, *Little Rock – Race and Resistance*, 188.
35. Thelma Mothershed Wair, personal interview conducted July 2013.
36. Frankie Muse Freeman with Candace O'Connor, *A Song of Faith and Hope – The Life of Frankie Muse Freeman*, 71-72.
37. Thelma Mothershed Wair, personal interview conducted July 2013.

Chapter 9

1. Thelma Mothershed Wair, personal interview conducted October 2006.
2. Ibid., Interview conducted July 2013.
3. J. Williams, *Eyes on the Prize*, 147-148, 155.
4. Nadine Cohodas, *The Band Played Dixie – Race and the Liberal Conscience at Ole Miss*, 84, and J. Williams, *Eyes on the Prize*, 195.
5. J. Williams, *Eyes on the Prize*, 184, 190.
6. Ibid., 195.
7. Thelma Mothershed Wair, personal interview conducted July 2013.
8. Margolick, *Elizabeth and Hazel*, 148.
9. *Nine From Little Rock*, Guggenheim Productions, Inc. for the United Information Agency. Written and directed by Charles Guggenheim, 1964.
10. Thelma Mothershed Wair, personal interviews conducted December 2011 and July 2013.
11. Ibid.
12. Ibid., Interview conducted December 2011.
13. Ibid., Interview conducted July 2013.
14. Ibid., Interview conducted December 2011.
15. Ibid.
16. Ibid., Interview conducted July 2013.

Chapter 10

1. Bill Clinton, "Remarks by the President in Ceremony Commemorating the 40th Anniversary of the Desegregation of Central High School," September 25, 1997, in Catherine Lewis and J. Richard Lewis (ed.), *Race, Politics, and Memory – A Documentary History of the Little Rock School Crisis*, 120.
2. Thelma Mothershed Wair, personal interview conducted December 2011.
3. Walls-LaNier, *A Mighty Long Way*, 247-248.
4. Thelma Mothershed Wair, personal interview conducted October 2006.
5. Ibid., Interview conducted December 2011.
6. Ibid.
7. John Leland and Vern E. Smith, "Echoes of Little Rock," *Newsweek*, Vol.130, No.13, September 29, 1997: 58.
8. Counts, *A Life is More Than a Moment*, 75.
9. Bill Clinton, Remarks by the President for the Congressional Gold Medal Ceremony for the Little Rock Nine, C-SPAN, November 9, 1999.
10. Thelma Mothershed Wair, personal interview conducted May 2009.
11. Ibid.
12. Ibid.
13. Ibid.
14. Ibid.
15. Ibid.
16. Walls-LaNier, *A Mighty Long Way*, 267.
17. Bill to Mint Coin Marking 50th Anniversary of LR Central High Desegregation Sent to President Bush, December 18, 2005, in *Race, Politics, and Memory*, 153.
18. Charlie Frago, "Once Again, Soldiers Conduct LR Nine In," *Arkansas Democrat-Gazette*, September 25, 2007: 4A.
19. Charlotte Tubbs and Heather Hahn, "Clinton: LR Nine Lessons Left to be Learned," *Arkansas Democrat-Gazette*, September 25, 2007: 1A, 4A.
20. Charlotte Tubbs, et al., "Still Far to Go, Nine Tell Central Crowd," *Arkansas Democrat-Gazette*, September 26, 2007: 1A.
21. Ibid, 4A.

Bibliography

Selected Books

Anderson, Karen. *Little Rock – Race and Resistance at Central High School*. Princeton: Princeton University Press, 2010.

Bates, Daisy. *The Long Shadow of Little Rock – A Memoir*. New York: David McKay Company, Inc., 1962.

Beals, Melba Patillo. *Warriors Don't Cry – A Searing Memoir of the Battle to Integrate Little Rock's Central High*. New York: Washington Square Press, 1994.

———. *White is a State of Mind – A Memoir*. New York: G. Putnam's Sons, 1999.

Blossom, Virgil T. *It HAS Happened Here*. New York: Harper & Brothers, 1959.

Branch, Taylor. *Parting the Waters – America in the King Years, 1954-1963*. New York: Touchstone, 1988.

Brewer, Vivion Lenon. *The Embattled Ladies of Little Rock: 1958-1963 – The Struggle to Save Public Education at Central High*. Fort Bragg: Lost Coast Press, 1999.

Brown, Robert R. *Bigger Than Little Rock*. Greenwich: The Seabury Press, 1958.

Childs, Marquis. *Eisenhower: Captive Hero*. New York: Harcourt, Brace & Co., 1958.

Cobb, James C. *The South and America Since World War II*. New York: Oxford University Press, 2012.

Cohodas, Nadine. *The Band Played Dixie – Race and the Liberal Conscience at Ole Miss*. New York: The Free Press, 1997.

Counts, I. Wilmer. *Life Is More Than a Moment – The Desegregation of Little Rock's Central High*. Bloomington: Indiana University Press, 1999.

DuBois, W. E. B. *The Souls of Black Folk*. New York: Barnes and Noble Books, 2003. Originally published by A. C. McClurg & Co., Chicago, 1903.

Dudziak, Mary L. *Cold War Civil Rights – Race and the Image of American Democracy*. Princeton: Princeton University Press, 2000.

Foner, Eric. *Reconstruction – America's Unfinished Revolution*. New York: Harper & Row, 1988.

Freeman, Frankie Muse with Candace O'Connor. *A Song of Faith and Hope – The Life of Frankie Muse Freeman*. St. Louis: Missouri Historical Society Press, 2003.

Gordon, Fon Louise. *Caste and Class – The Black Experience in Arkansas, 1880-1920*. Athens: University of Georgia Press, 1995.

Gordy, Sondra. *Finding the Lost Year – What Happened When Little Rock Closed Its Public Schools*. Fayetteville: University of Arkansas Press, 2009.

Hays, Brooks. *A Southern Moderate Speaks*. Chapel Hill: University of North Carolina Press, 1959.

Huckaby, Elizabeth. *Crisis at Central High – Little Rock, 1957-58*. Baton Rouge: Louisiana State University Press, 1980.

Jackson, Kenneth T. *The Ku Klux Klan in the City, 1915-1930*. New York: Oxford University Press, 1967.

Jacoway, Elizabeth. *Turn Away Thy Son – Little Rock, the Crisis that Shocked the Nation*. New York: Free Press, 2007.

Jacoway, Elizabeth and C. Fred Williams (ed.). *Understanding the Little Rock Crisis – An Exercise in Remembrance and Reconciliation*. Fayetteville: The University of Arkansas Press, 1999.

Johnson, Ben F. *Arkansas in Modern America – 1930-1999*. Fayetteville: The University of Arkansas Press, 2000.

Johnson, Haynes and Harry Katz. *Herblock – The Life and Work of the Great Political Cartoonist*. New York: W. W. Norton & Co., 2009.

Kirk, John A. *Redefining the Color Line – Black Activism in Little Rock, Arkansas, 1940-1970*. Gainesville: University Press of Florida, 2002.

Lewis, Catherine and J. Richard Lewis (ed.). *Race, Politics, and Memory – A Documentary History of the Little Rock School Crisis*. Fayetteville: University of Arkansas Press, 2007.

Little Rock U.S.A. – Materials for Analysis. San Francisco: Chandler Publishing Company, Inc., 1960.

Margolick, David. *Elizabeth and Hazel – Two Women Of Little Rock*. New Haven: Yale University Press, 2011.

Martin, Waldo E., Jr. *Brown v. Board of Education – A Brief History with Documents*. Boston: Bedford/St. Martin's Press, 1998.

McWhirter, Cameron. *Red Summer – The Summer of 1919 and the Awakening of Black America*. New York: Henry Holt and Co. Inc., 2011.

Medley, Keith Weldon. *We As Freemen – Plessy v. Ferguson*. Gretna: Pelican Publishers, 2003.

Murphy, Sara. *Breaking the Silence – Little Rock's Women's Emergency Committee to Open Our Schools, 1958-1963*. Fayetteville: The University of Arkansas Press, 1997.

National Association for the Advancement of Colored People. *Thirty Years of Lynching in the United States, 1889-1918*. New York: NAACP, 1919 (reprinted 2010).

Packard, Jerrold. *American Nightmare – The History of Jim Crow*. New York: St. Martin's Press, 2002.

Pietrusza, David. *1948 – Harry Truman's Improbable Victory and the Year That Transformed America*. New York: Union Square Press, 2011.

Polakow, Amy. *Daisy Bates – Civil Rights Crusader*. North Haven: Linnet Books, 2003.

Reed, Roy. *Faubus – The Life and Times of an American Prodigal*. Fayetteville: University of Arkansas Press, 1997.

Ritterhouse, Jennifer. *Growing Up Jim Crow – How Black and White Children Learned Race*. Chapel Hill: University of North Carolina Press, 2006.

Roberts, Terrence. *Lessons from Little Rock*. Little Rock: Butler Center Books, 2009.

Roy, Beth. *Bitters in the Honey – Tales of Hope and Disappointment Across Divides of Race and Time*. Fayetteville: The University of Arkansas Press, 1999.

Shufeldt, Robert W. *The Negro – A Menace to American Civilization*. Boston: Gorham Press, 1907.

Strausbaugh, John. *Black Like You – Blackface, Whiteface, Insult and Imitation in American Popular Culture*. New York: Penguin Books, 2006.

Wade, Wyn Craig. *The Fiery Cross – The Ku Klux Klan in America*. New York: Oxford University Press, 1987.

Walls-LaNier, Carlotta. *A Mighty Long Way – My Journey to Justice at Little Rock Central High School*. New York: One World, 2009.

Williams, Juan. *Eyes on the Prize – America's Civil Rights Years, 1954-1965*. New York: Penguin Books, 1987.

Woodward, C. Vann. *The Strange Career of Jim Crow*. New York: Oxford University Press, 1957.

Selected Magazines, Journals

"The Battle of Nashville," *TIME*. Vol.70, No.13, September 23, 1957, 14-15.

Cope, Graeme. "A Note on Crowds during the Little Rock Crisis," *Arkansas Historical Quarterly*. Vol.67, No.3, Autumn 2008, 245-267.

"An Historic Week of Civil Strife," *LIFE*. Vol.43, No.15, October 7, 1957, 39-48.

Jacoway, Elizabeth. "Not Anger but Sorrow: Minnijean Brown Trickey Remembers the Little Rock Crisis," *Arkansas Historical Quarterly*. Vol.64, No.1 Spring 2005, 21-23.

Knebel, Fletcher. "The Real Story of Little Rock," *LOOK*. Vol.21, No.23, November 12, 1957, 31-37.

Leland, John and Vern E. Smith. "Echoes of Little Rock," *Newsweek*. Vol.130, No.13, September 29, 1997, 52-58.

"The Meaning of Little Rock," *TIME*. Vol.70, No.15, October 7, 1957, 21-25.

"A 'Morally Right' Decision," *LIFE*. Vol.39 No.4, July 25, 1955, 29-31.

"Retreat from Newport," *TIME*. Vol.70, No.13, September 23, 1957, 11.

"What Orval Hath Wrought," *TIME*. Vol.70, No.13, September 23, 1957, 13.

Selected Newspaper Articles

"9 Negroes Enter Second Week at Central High School Under Guard," *Arkansas State Press*, October 4, 1957, 1.

"Central High Quiet As Negroes Fail to Show," *Arkansas Democrat*, September 24, 1957: A1.

"CHS Emptied by Bomb Scare Shortly After U.S. Troops Force Integration," *Arkansas Democrat*, September 25, 1957: A1.

"The Crisis Mr. Faubus Made," *Arkansas Gazette*, September 4, 1957: A1.

Frago, Charlie. "Once Again, Soldiers Conduct LR Nine In," *Arkansas Democrat-Gazette*, September 25, 2007: 4A.

"North Little Rock Whites Bar School to 6 Negroes," *New York Times*, September 10, 1957: A1.

"Nothing Much Happened," *Arkansas Democrat*, September 23, 1957: A1.

"Riot in Little Rock," *Detroit News*, September 23, 1957: 1-2.

"School Quiet, Attendance Rises As Week Closes at Little Rock," *Atlantic City Press*, September 28, 1957: A1.

Tubbs, Charlotte. "Event Sets Clock Ticking on Central Anniversary," *Arkansas Democrat Gazette*, May 21, 2006: B1.

Tubbs, Charlotte and Heather Hahn. "Clinton: LR Nine Lessons Left to be Learned," *Arkansas Democrat-Gazette*, September 25, 2007: 1A, 4A.

Tubbs, Charlotte, et al. "Still Far to Go, Nine Tell Central Crowd," *Arkansas Democrat-Gazette*, September 26, 2007: 1A, 4A.

"Two Men Hurt Today in Clash With the Troops at Little Rock," *Leominster Daily Enterprise*, September 25, 1957: A1.

"Two Negro Students Reported Beaten at CHS; Others Jeered," *Arkansas Democrat*, October 2, 1957: A1.

"Whites Treat Negro Pupils Friendly," *Arkansas Democrat*, September 25, 1957: A1.

Miscellaneous Documents

Arrangements for Students, December 1958. Reprinted from *Southern School News*, January 1959, 14 in *LRUSA*, 132.

Bill Clinton, "Remarks by the President in Ceremony Commemorating the 40th Anniversary of the Desegregation of Central High School," September 25, 1997, in *Race, Politics, and Memory – A Documentary History of the Little Rock School Crisis*, 120.

Georgia Governor at Segregationist Dinner, August 22, 1957. Reprinted from *Southern School News*, September 1957, 7 in *LRUSA*, 32-33.

"The Governor's Explanation," September 2, 1957. Reprinted from *Southern School News*, October 1957, 1 in *LRUSA*, 37.

Godfrey, Phoebe Christina. "Sweet Little Girls? Miscegenation, Desegregation and the Defense of Whiteness at Little Rock's Central High, 1957-1959." PhD dissertation, Binghamton University, New York, 2001.

Interview with Student Leader in Central High School, September 1957. Reprinted from the *Arkansas Gazette*, September 10, 1957, 4A in *LRUSA*, 43.

"Legal Moves to Block Integration – August 29-30, 1957." Reprinted from *Southern School News*, September 1957, 6 in *LRUSA*, 34-35.

Little Rock Board of Education. Petition to U.S. Dist. Ct. E. Ark., September 3, 1957. Reprinted from *Race Relations Law Reporter*, October 1957, 937-938 in *LRUSA*, 38.

President Eisenhower's speech to the nation, September 24, 1957, Reprinted in *LRUSA*, 64-66.

Provisions of New Schools Acts by Arkansas State Legislature, Reprinted from *Southern School News*, September 1958, 4 in *LRUSA*, 114-115.

Re-election of Governor Faubus, July 29, 1958. Reprinted from *New York Times*, July 30, 1958, 1, 14 in *LRUSA*, 105.

Telegram sent by Governor Faubus to President Eisenhower, September 4, 1957. Reprinted from the *Southern School News*, October 1957, 1-2, in *LRUSA*, 39.

Government Documents/Supreme Court Cases

Arkansas Black Code Sec.5 (1867).
Brown et al. v. Board of Education of Topeka et al., 349 U.S. 294 (1955).
McLaurin v. Oklahoma State Regents for Higher Education et al., 339 U.S. 637 (1950).
Plessy v. Ferguson, 163 U.S. 537 (1896).
Southern Manifesto, 102 Cong. Rec. 4515-16 (1956).
Sweatt v. Painter, 339 U.S. 629 (1950).

Films/Video

Congressional Gold Medal Ceremony for the Little Rock Nine, *C-SPAN*, aired November 9, 1999.
Eyes on the Prize (PBS/Blackside Productions), 1987.
The Lost Year – The Untold Story of the Year Following the Crisis at Central High School (Morning Star Studio), 2007.
Nine From Little Rock, Guggenheim Productions Inc. for the United Information Agency. Written and directed by Charles Guggenheim, 1964.
"Where Are They Now?" *NBC – The Today Show*, aired February 1, 2002.

Selected Archival Material

Central High School National Historic Site Collections, Little Rock, Arkansas
Eisenhower Presidential Library Special Collections, Abilene, Kansas
University of Arkansas at Little Rock Library Special Collections, Little Rock, Arkansas

Personal Interviews

Thelma Mothershed Wair. Conducted September 2001, July 2003, October 2006, May 2007, December 2011, October 2012, July 2013, and January 2014.
Ernest Green. Conducted January 2002.
Elizabeth Eckford. Conducted July 2003.
Minnijean Brown-Trickey. Conducted July 2003.
Gilbert Mothershed. Conducted December 2011 (phone).
Michael and Lucille Mothershed. Conducted December 2011 and October 2012.
Lois Mothershed-Pot. Conducted January and May 2012 (phone/email).
Terrence Roberts. Conducted November 2013.
Grace Mothershed Davis. Conducted August 2014 (phone).